about the
Authors

The authors of this book represent well over 150 years of Career and Technical Education (CTE) experience and come from a broad range of perspectives and position specialties within that field. In addition, the contributing authors represent another 100 years, totaling 250 years altogether.

Dr. Belinda Cole has a background of wide-ranging experience, from being a school counselor in junior high and high school settings to working at the Oklahoma Department of Career and Technology Education. She is now teaching and researching at the university level. Belinda was a health teacher who went on to earn her master's degree in school guidance and counseling, along with a license as an Oklahoma Licensed Professional Counselor; she is also a nationally certified counselor. She became the State Guidance Coordinator at the Oklahoma Department of Career and Technology Education and held that position for over 10 years. She was promoted to Associate State Director

4

Your First Year in CTE:

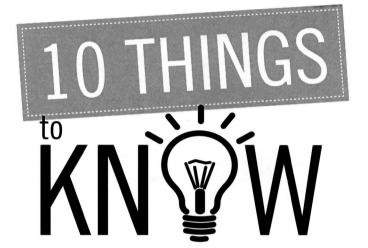

to 10 THINGS to KNOW

ISBN# 978-0-692-30134-0

Published by the Association for Career
and Technical Education

1410 King Street Alexandria, VA 22314
Phone: 800-826-9972 // Fax: 703-683-7424
www.acteonline.org // *Connecting Education and Careers*

Table of Contents

and served in that role for 11 years. Belinda was offered a unique opportunity to serve at Oklahoma State University as Associate Professor and Francis Tuttle Endowed Chair for Workforce and Adult Education in 2008. She served in that role until 2014, teaching CTE teachers, administrators, and business and industry trainers in the master's and Ph.D. programs. Dr. Cole coordinated and was lead instructor for a fast-track program for new CTE teachers direct from industry. She served on the National Assessment of Career and Technical Education (NACTE) panel and is currently the Fellows Leadership Program Coordinator for the Association for Career and Technical Education (ACTE). She is also currently the facilitator for the ACTE-ECMC Foundation Postsecondary Leadership Success Program.

Dr. John Foster's career experience began when he was a tradesman in the construction industry. In the early years of the Vocational Education Acts, a community college career counselor had John visit a carpentry program in a regional school. Soon after that visit he began his career in CTE as a carpentry teacher. At the time, John was a bit of a rarity: he had a bachelor's degree in vocational education as a starting teacher. He later earned a master's degree in vocational education administration and became a CTE director at the secondary level. John completed a Ph.D. in workforce development and began work in CTE teacher education. It was in these two positions that he became aware of the positive power of instructional improvement through the objective use of data. Dr. Foster took a position as a state director of CTE and served three different governors. Dr. Foster also formed relationships with a number of key researchers in the field of CTE; among them, Dr. Ken Gray, Dr. Neil (Mac) McCaslin, and Dr. James Stone. John credits the many stars of CTE that he has met along the way for sharing their expertise and hopes his experiences will benefit those reading this book. In 2005, Dr. Foster took the helm of NOCTI, formerly the National Occupational Competency Testing Institute, and while there has forged strong ties with Advance CTE, formerly NASDCTEc (state directors of CTE), and ACTE.

Dr. Pamela Foster obtained her bachelor's and master's degrees in science education and later obtained a Ph.D. in workforce education and development. She taught in a comprehensive (academic and CTE) high school for 34 years, during which she was also the science program chair for twelve years. As a science representative, Pam worked with and mentored academic and CTE educators to create motivating, integrated lessons and units. She has shared her experiences and practices at local, state, and national conferences. Pam has also facilitated webinars for the Southern Regional Education Board (SREB) and was responsible for planning integrated nationwide professional development activities as well. She was recognized in 1991 as a semi-finalist for state teacher of the year and was recognized as the outstanding biology teacher in 2010 by the state of Pennsylvania. Now retired, Pam continues to mentor new CTE teachers and volunteers with the Audubon Society in teaching grade-school students about STEM-related issues, including stream ecology and conservation.

Dr. Kathleen McNally is a school improvement specialist for SREB, specifically working with high schools and technical centers to operationalize the *Technology Centers That Work* (TCTW) Ten Key Practices and Key Conditions. She has worked as a high school mathematics teacher, as the Associate Director of Training for national SkillsUSA, in higher education in a university workforce education and development program as a CTE Teacher Educator, and as the Director of CTE for the Milton Hershey School. Kathleen has worked with new and seasoned CTE teachers while partnering with them as colleagues on student projects and assignments and supporting them in their quest for teacher certification. She has helped teachers in the role of student organization advisors to navigate the challenges and rewards of being Career Technical Student Organization (CTSO) advisors. Kathleen's work with SREB involves working with states on embedding mathematics into CTE instruction, including facilitating the adoption of the Mathematics Design Collaborative (MDC) tools and frameworks, working with faculties on embracing Project-Based Learning (PBL) instructional/planning approaches, and facilitating TCTW and *High Schools That Work* (HSTW) efforts across the network.

setting the
Stage

CTE teachers are a special breed. Over the years, the authors have worked in the field of CTE and have not only witnessed this "specialness" but have also served in various capacities within the field itself (teachers, administrators, state officials, mentors, teacher educators, board members, and advisory boards). We wrote these chapters not only with the hope that they would continue to help the CTE community grow and prosper, but also because we believe deeply in CTE and its many positive impacts.

This book is specific to CTE teachers because, unlike most other teachers, a majority of CTE teachers don't come to teaching via a college teaching degree. If they come with a degree, many times it is from a field that is not education related. In many states this is referred to as an "alternate route"; in CTE, this is the common route. This career trajectory brings with it distinct differences. Here are a few of them.

- A CTE teacher often starts his or her teaching career at an older age than most teachers of regular education.
- CTE teachers typically have many years of content experience before entering the classroom.
- CTE teachers make a substantial career change to enter the classroom. Many times they are at the top of their particular field, and they transition into a career they know little about, starting over at the bottom rung.
- CTE teachers make a commitment to a lifetime of education. Not only do they have to maintain currency with the technical field that they left, but they must also play "catch up" in their new field. In many states, alternatively credentialed CTE teachers have to acquire a substantial number of college credits in teaching pedagogy while simultaneously working in a new field.

These four differences alone create a ripple effect that makes it more difficult for such CTE teachers to navigate their new environment.

Without proper support, some of these difficulties may cause those entering their new field to give up and return to their former field. Even those with support and a good initial "launch" may end up working so hard to succeed that burnout becomes a real issue. The research literature and folklore surrounding CTE teaching indicate that this attrition occurs in the first three to four years for those new to CTE teaching.

This book, then, is meant to be an easy and fun read for newer CTE teachers, especially those who begin without any background in education, but it should be a great resource for veteran CTE teachers too. The hands-on examples can also provide teachers in regular education classrooms with ideas that can be adapted for their classrooms. Not only do we want this to be one of those books you'll enjoy reading, but we also hope that you will keep the information, examples, and resources nearby for use in your teaching.

We know CTE teachers are a special breed, and if you are new to our field, we want to welcome you to what we hope becomes your new passion as it did for us.

chapter I
Learning the Language of CTE
What the Heck Does That Mean?

You have made a commitment to become a CTE teacher, and in "Setting the Stage," you found out that you are part of a special breed. You are dedicated to maintaining currency with two distinct content areas—your area of technical expertise and this new content of teaching. Chances are good that you don't need any help with your technical content, but the teaching piece, well, that's a different story! All of us probably remember our first day on the job, in the lab or clinic, and that may be a scary memory with so many new and different things—new people, new instruments, and different equipment. You may quickly experience that in the world of education, there also seems to be a different language—these terms, acronyms, and strange sayings can be quite foreign and can certainly be confusing!

Let's take a look at this new language in action as we join Mr. Neuteach for one of his first days in the classroom. After the story, we'll fill you in on what all these strange terms mean and how they can be beneficial to you as a new CTE teacher!

It is a beautiful fall morning, and Mr. Neuteach pulls into what already seems to be his permanent parking spot at the Students-R-Stars Technical Center, with a warm cup of his favorite morning beverage. He unloads his folders with the paperwork he was reviewing the night before, including some student IEPs, a memo from the director on professional development on PBL and SSR, and information on a website that his mentor asked him to read on Advance CTE and its resources. The director also wanted teachers to think about a possible capstone project for next year that reflects the new POS and Career Pathways for his program. Mr. Neuteach has arrived early so he can settle into his classroom and lab and have a moment to say hello to his fellow teachers before students arrive. A short faculty meeting is also scheduled. He stops at his mailbox to pull out a flyer about the school's CTSO fundraiser, an application for ACTE membership, and a memo with a schedule of testing dates for the NOCTI Technical Skills Assessment.

The director, who has a reputation for being sharp, involved, and fast-moving, is heading quickly toward the faculty workroom with a handful of meeting agendas. Mr. Neuteach sees the director give another teacher a tap on the shoulder and hears him say, "Super job yesterday, Mr. Experienced! Great activation strategy! Loved your engaging PowerPoint presentation on the smartboard for the lesson and the way you handled your students' questions about calculating the bend in the pipe by summarizing with those student whiteboards. I was really impressed with your use of formative assessment, the rubric for the next project, and that clever ticket-out-the-door activity. I also appreciate your bell-to-bell teaching approach; it sends a great message to your students that you want them to be successful!" And off he dashes, while Mr. Neuteach takes in the compliments given to the other teacher.

"Good morning. How are you, Mr. Neuteach?" cheerfully calls Mr. Chip Woodcraft from the hallway. "Would you like to join us for lunch today? We're ordering grinders in from the local spot on the corner and watching a TeacherTube video on 21st century skills. It's going to be emphasized on our new state performance assessment, so we want to get ahead of the game!"

"Thanks, Chip, I'd like to join you ... appreciate the offer! Hey, if you don't mind me asking, can you shed some light on something for me? What is a grinder?"

Let's take a quick look at Mr. Neuteach's strange, terminology-packed morning and see if we can help with some definitions. We alphabetized the terms from our story above so that you can find them more easily later.

Building Your Knowledge

21st Century Skills: These skills are also known as workplace readiness skills, success skills, employability skills, foundational skills, or soft skills. These skill sets are defined by many groups, but basically refer to general skills needed by all employees. Examples would include attributes like cooperation, teamwork, and ethical decision-making. Good examples of these kinds of skills can be found in the Department of Labor's Competency Models Clearinghouse at https://www.careeronestop.org/CompetencyModel/Competency-Models/pyramid-home.aspx, usually distributed under tiers one through three.

ACTE (Association for Career and Technical Education): It is the largest national education association dedicated to the advancement of education that prepares youth and adults for careers and provides leadership in developing a competitive workforce.

Activation Strategy: This strategy is often called an anticipatory set, hook, or bell ringer. This is a teaching strategy to capture and focus the students' attention on the upcoming lesson. It must pique their interest and should continue only long enough to get them excited about the lesson objective. This strategy can be used not only at the beginning of a class, but also at any time a different activity or new concept is to be introduced. One example of an activation strategy could be to show a picture of a piece of equipment, perhaps an engine lathe, and see if any students know what it is called, what it is used for, and who might be able to identify any of its parts.

Advance CTE (formerly known as National Association of State Directors of Career Technical Education Consortium): This organization was established in 1920 to represent the state and territory heads of secondary, postsecondary, and adult CTE across the nation. It aims to support an innovative CTE system that cultivates best practices and speaks with a collective voice on national policy to promote academic and technical excellence that ensures a career-ready workforce in a global, dynamic economy.

Bell-to-bell: This is a teaching strategy that maximizes learning time from the beginning of the class period to the end (bell-to-bell). All class activities should relate to the objectives of the lesson and move students toward the theme or big idea of the content being studied.

Capstone: Used to describe a culminating activity that usually involves a larger project or presentation that demonstrates multiple competencies students have acquired.

Career Pathways: A combination of rigorous and high-quality education, training, and other services that aligns with the skill needs of industries in the economy of the state or regional economy involved and prepares an individual to be successful in any of a full range of secondary or postsecondary education options. These pathways should also include counseling and education offered in the same context as one would find in the workplace. Lastly, the pathway should enable individuals to obtain a diploma and a recognized postsecondary credential which will help them advance within a specific occupation.

CTSO: Career and Technical Student Organizations are co-curricular voluntary student associations that focus on leadership development in addition to technical content. Examples of student organizations include FFA (formerly the Future Farmers of America), SkillsUSA (specializing in technical education programs), Future Business Leaders of America (FBLA), and a number of others. Learn more at CTSOs.org.

Director: A director is the instructional and administrative leader in a secondary school or school district delivering CTE courses. An individual with this title generally has specific state certifications and board-level responsibilities in addition to maintaining instructional leadership.

Faculty meeting: Faculty meetings are typically a mandatory gathering of CTE and other school professionals, generally called in advance by a school administrator. These can occur prior to or at the conclusion of a school day, or they could occur prior to or after a school year. The focus of these meetings could be operational or instructional.

Formative assessment: With a goal focus of providing feedback to a CTE teacher regarding student competency development, formative assessments are usually some sort of test or quiz. Information gained provides opportunities for teachers to make adjustments in the ways they deliver instruction.

Grinder: Also known as subs, submarine sandwiches, or hoagies, grinders are a favorite lunchtime sandwich, sometimes toasted, that contains a variety of tasty meats and vegetables. Are you getting hungry yet?

IEP: Individual Education Plans are mandated by the Individuals with Disabilities Education Act (IDEA). An IEP defines the individualized objectives of a student who has been found to have a disability (as defined by federal regulations). Its intention is to help those with disabilities to reach educational goals more easily than they might otherwise, and it must be tailored to the individual's needs.

NOCTI: Formerly known as the National Occupational Competency Testing Institute, NOCTI is a leading provider of high-quality technical competency assessment products and services for secondary and post-secondary educational institutions. NOCTI provides nationally recognized credentialing assessments in well over 150 technical areas.

PBL: Project-Based Learning is a student-centered, active learning style that engages students to learn about a subject through the experience of problem-solving. Students are also exposed to self-directed learning with incorporated collaboration skills, increasing motivation.

POS: Programs of Study are a coordinated, nonduplicative sequence of academic and technical content at the secondary or postsecondary level that incorporates challenging state standards; addresses both academic and technical knowledge and skills, including employability skills; is aligned with the needs of industry in the economy of the state, region, tribal community, or local area; progresses in specificity (beginning with all aspects of an industry or career cluster and leading to more occupational-specific instruction); has multiple entry and exit points that incorporate credentialing; culminates in the attainment of a recognized postsecondary credential; and leads to an industry-recognized credential such as an associate or bachelor's degree, a postsecondary certificate, or an industry certification. The Strengthening Career and Technical Education for the 21st Century (Perkins V) is the major source of federal funding for CTE.

PowerPoint presentation: A term coined by Microsoft based on its software program, PowerPoint. PowerPoint uses a series of slides that incorporate text, pictures, tables, charts, animations, short videos, and/or links to internet sites. PowerPoint helps educators to present the targeted content of their lesson objectives to students in an organized, interesting, and effective manner.

Rubric: A means of communicating expectations for an assignment, a rubric clarifies the standards for a quality performance (as with a project) and provides focused feedback on works in progress and helps grade final products.

SSR: Also known as Sustained Silent Reading, this strategy encourages school-based recreational, voluntary reading in which students read silently at a designated time period during school. CTE students usually choose areas related to their content. This strategy increases knowledge and develops good reading habits as well.

Smartboard: A smartboard is an electronic interactive white screen that is tied to a computer and uses touch detection for user input in the same way that a tablet device is used. In education, a smartboard can be utilized to show a teacher's digital presentations to students.

TeacherTube: An online community of educators sharing instructional videos and content, TeacherTube is a free-to-use resource and is touted as a "safe" venue for teachers, schools, and home learners.

Technical Center: Technical centers are also known as Area Vocational Technical Schools, Career Technical Centers, Regional Occupational Programs, and by numerous others titles. Separate facilities housing technical skill training are often used cooperatively by a number of high schools so that expensive equipment and expertise can be shared. Technical centers may also provide CTE to adults.

Technical Skills Assessment: Technical skill assessments or end-of-program assessments are instruments, often from a third party, that provide a summative assessment of a CTE student's technical knowledge and skills. These assessments were required under Perkins IV for assessing CTE student technical skill attainment and numerous states are now utilizing the data generated by their use to determine secondary and postsecondary program performance under Perkins V

Ticket-Out-the-Door: Also known as an exit ticket, this is a teaching strategy used by teachers to collect written feedback from students about the day's learning prior to students leaving the classroom. Tickets can be as simple as a piece of paper with an important question about the lesson's key concept. This helps the teacher determine if content was understood.

Whiteboards: Whiteboards or individualized student response boards are utilized by teachers to check for immediate student understanding and to immediately display feedback to the teacher and/or students by answering questions, making drawings, showing calculations, and so forth. Effective for student summarizing and clarifying information, whiteboards may be used individually, with markers, or could be an electronic system.

All right, so there you have some definitions and terminology that you may hear in the first few days on your new job! We hope you have them all memorized! We also want to let you in on a little secret. The rest of the chapters in this little handbook are laid out differently than this first chapter. What we've tried to do is keep the chapters as short and fun as possible, and very useful and easy to understand. The chapters ahead provide a few pages of content, followed by some experiences from the field and some key points and citations for additional resources. We hope you enjoy the book, but more than that, we hope you are beginning a long and successful career as a CTE teacher!

Experiences from the field

This chapter was really about definitions, and one of the definitions mentioned was a ticket-out-the-door. One of the strategies that could be used is an exit slip. This example comes to us from one of our friends in Kentucky.

Have you ever given a test and the results left you saying to your colleagues, "I taught it, but they didn't learn it?" Every teacher struggles with helping students master the academic and technical competencies required for students to be successful and earn a valued credential. Some teachers wait until all of the material has been presented and use a summative assessment at the end to measure progress. Effective teachers measure students' progress along the way using formative assessments to monitor student growth. Formative assessments can vary depending on when they are used during the class. If a teacher is lecturing, randomly calling on students to answer questions is a formative assessment tool. A simple strategy used at the end of class to close the lesson is an exit slip, or ticket-out-the-door. A question is provided and students write their answers on a piece of paper and turn it in as they leave the class. This formative assessment technique engages all students and provides the all-important evidence of student learning for a teacher.

How do you know what to ask in an exit slip? As you plan your lessons, you are creating learning objectives to provide a clear focus for the day's lesson. By posting and explaining the objective, you are sharing with the students what they will learn. For example, the competency might be "We will review lab/shop safety practices and procedures." The exit slip allows you to close the lesson as a reflection on if the students learned the content. The exit slip for the lesson could be: "List three safety practices that are required in all manufacturing plants that we will use in our lab daily." As students leave the classroom, collect and read the slips to determine if the students mastered the objective!

RELATED CONTENT THAT MAY BE OF INTEREST

Association for Career Technical Education. (2019a). *Career and technical student organizations*. Alexandria, VA: ACTE. Available at https://www.acteonline.org/professional-development/high-quality-cte-tools/career-and-technical-student-organizations/.

CareerOneStop. (2019a). *Generic Building Blocks Competency Model*. Washington, DC: US Department of Labor, Employment and Training Administration. Available at https://www.careeronestop.org/CompetencyModel/competency-models/building-blocks-model.aspx.

Fiscus, L. (ed) & Hyslop, A. (2008). *Career and technical student organizations reference guide*. Leesburg, VA: SkillsUSA. Available at https://www.skillsusa.org/wp-content/uploads/2014/12/CTSOs-a-Reference-Guide.pdf.

chapter II
The Teacher as a Role Model
Sign a Modeling Contract

Teacher as a role model and mentor

When you were growing up, what did you want to be? Perhaps you wanted to be a fireman, an astronaut, or maybe a famous actor or a model. The authors of this book believe that when you signed on to be a CTE teacher, you signed that modeling contract; congratulations! You are probably wondering how you can teach and be a role model. Well, the reality and the research indicate that if you are teaching students about 21st century skills for success in a career, you are one of the most influential models students can follow. Being a role model is like being on stage or in the spotlight with your students as your audience. Just as young children watch and learn from everything you do, so too do high school students and even adults. Nowadays, the "spotlight" is quite large and shines 24/7. Chapter V: Establishing Student-Teacher Boundaries offers some advice on relating to students in your new role.

Part of your modeling contract entails making every effort to:

- Listen to your students
- Focus on their needs
- Build professional supportive relationships
- Be sensitive to differences
- Be realistic
- Offer guidance

Another part of your modeling contract involves knowing your audience. Generally speaking, a new CTE teacher may be a bit removed from that audience in terms of experience and age. Don't worry, we've provided a quick primer to understand some of the current generations with which you may be working.

Many experts point out that Generation X, Y, and Z students, those born from 1966 to the present, have a slightly different background and expectations from other generations of students you may have associated with growing up. On average, these genera-tions, including the most recent generation, Z, are confident beyond their years and have taken on the role of  teaching their elders how to make technology work. They believe in their skills and are not shy about taking risks. (Beall, 2017; Schroer, n.d.). They want the direction and support that adults and employers can provide, but they are also looking for the freedom to get the task done at their own pace, utilizing their own creativity. Generation X, Y, and Z students are a walking contradiction in that they can be independent, but they also possess an intense desire for collaboration.

The payoff for your role modeling is worth the investment. Most students tend to thrive when surrounded by good role models. CTE teachers also have a unique opportunity to work with their students over a lengthy period of time, often up to three years. This allows for you to add another important role to your résumé—that of a mentor. A mentor is an experienced and trusted person who gives another person advice and help. As a teacher, a mentor is someone who takes a special interest in helping another person to develop into a successful professional.

A mentoring relationship develops over an extended period, during which a student's needs and the nature of the relationship tend to change. A mentor will try to be aware of these changes and vary the degree and type of attention, help, advice, information, and encouragement offered.

Teacher-mentors who engage with their students and encourage them to develop, take responsibility for their actions, own their goals, and be

 self-reliant are likely to be more successful than those who set out to "save" or "fix" their students with a more prescriptive approach. Partnering to help students shape their career is a powerful position. Often CTE teachers spend more time with their students than the students' own parents have the opportunity to do. That makes you, the CTE teacher, very important in a student's professional development.

A teacher-mentor is someone students believe in, respect, and honor. Teacher-mentors are regarded by students as honest, sincere, loyal, and genuine; have high credibility; are reliable and true to what they believe is right; and are prepared to accept and acknowledge personal responsibility for their actions. Such teachers are sought after by students looking for role models.

Students value a teacher-mentor who is an authority figure, and who can also model these attributes:

- Embodies wisdom, trustworthiness, and dependability; someone wise, trusted, and dependable who can still be an authority figure
- Helps students express themselves assertively in emotional situations, rather than aggressively or passively
- Encourages a nonjudgmental relationship
- Seeks to empower students with key life skills
- Assists with a student's daily improvement
- Provides honest and constructive encouragement

You'll find more information about some things that you should and should not do in Chapter V: Establishing Student-Teacher Boundaries.

Experiences from the field

We talked to an agriculture teacher in West Virginia who offers a unique "trick" to not only personalize the learning for his students, but also give them the opportunity to help someone they care about. This is sometimes referred to as "service learning." Regardless of the terminology, this kind of opportunity allows students to mature and continue to develop a sense of self-worth. This teacher invited his students to ask around among their family and friends to see if anyone was having trouble with any equipment that was powered by a small engine. The class held a meeting to compile the list of potential jobs. The instructor helped students organize this information so that the jobs lined up with the sequence of his curriculum. He then had students invite their friends and relatives to bring their piece of equipment at a designated time to take advantage of the group's services to fix the problems, and he named the student who found the job the manager. A construction teacher from Kentucky used a similar service-learning approach but tapped the entire community for potential customers. His students were able to work at a local elementary school helping to create an outdoor classroom while demonstrating some of their skills to younger students. Both activities provided multiple growth and leadership opportunities for students.

Many experienced CTE teachers balance the pressures of their modeling contract by using stories of their experiences mixed with a sense of humor. We found a team of teachers in New York who created a fun business card which included their pictures and school contact information. The card was distributed to their students (and parents). This not only sent a message that they were accessible, but it also demonstrated that they were in control of the type of information they shared. As a role model, you may find students asking for advice on anything from guidance on career choices and postsecondary education, to questions that are more personal in nature such as friend or family relationships.

We have observed teachers who share life philosophies in order to invite students to contemplate their own philosophies. For example, a buildings trade teacher in Pennsylvania was often heard telling his students, "Remember, your character is defined by your actions," or "If you were the boss, would you hire you?" as a way to encourage students to not only reflect on their choices, but also to own their decisions. Personal stories about fellow workers (names withheld) or customers can be engaging and a great learning tool.

With all the focus on agreements between secondary and postsecondary CTE programs, referred to as articulations, many schools invite community college or technical college representatives into their classrooms; these individuals can also describe opportunities for students completing their program of study. This gives students an opportunity to visualize a potential career path, and in your role as mentor, helps them to see the goalpost at the end of the field.

Another "trick" that works well in today's job market is to help students open doors by diversifying skill development and taking advantage of all opportunities that provide quality learning. Students can benefit from observing that you use a professional network and value training (informal and formal). Think about inviting your professional colleagues, advisory committee members, and local industry and postsecondary representatives to participate in end-of-the-year interviews with your students to provide feedback, advisement, and real-world job-seeking experience. Think of yourself as a matchmaker between your students and valuable resources to help them navigate their career paths.

A cooperative arrangement in Illinois serves 500 students in a partnership between two school districts. A mentoring program began in

2003 with teachers volunteering their participation in the first two years. In the beginning, students and teachers met over lunch to talk about issues of interest and importance. Currently, every teacher participates by mentoring a group of no more than 15 students through four years of high school. Students are grouped alphabetically. The groups meet in their homeroom daily for 10 minutes and once a month for 30 minutes between third and fourth periods.

Teacher-mentors facilitate grade-specific lessons and arrange for guest speakers, especially for seniors. The programs demonstrate to students that teachers want to work with them to get the most out of high school and to prepare them for the future. The mentoring lessons for each grade level include the following topics:

- Designing a counseling system to ensure students take the right courses for achieving education and career goals
- Championing students to achieve at higher levels and graduate

Additional mentoring topics by year include:

Freshmen:
- A student council speaker and a handbook quiz
- Participating in a career interest inventory
- How well do you know your school?
- Letter writing
- Nonverbal communication

Sophomores:
- Exam preparation
- Job applications and interview practices
- Work ethic
- Review of the school handbook

Juniors:
- Brainstorming skills for the real world and job shadowing
- Grade Point Average (GPA), transcripts, and scholarship information
- Stress and time management

Seniors:
- Practice preparing college and scholarship applications
- College countdown, college costs, GPA, and transcripts
- Identity theft and credit cards
- Job applications, résumés, and an interview packet
- Cooperative learning experiences
- Soft skills/employability skills discussion

KEY POINTS FROM THIS CHAPTER

1. Being a role model is rewarding.
2. Think about what your students see in your modeling.
3. Help students see and weigh choices.
4. Build professional relationships with students.
5. Be aware of the needs of each student you are mentoring.

RELATED CONTENT THAT MAY BE OF INTEREST

Beall, G. (2017, November 6). Eight Key differences between Gen Z and Millennials. Verizon Media, Huffpost. Available at https://www.huffpost.com/entry/8-key-differences-between_b_12814200.

Mentor Michigan. (n.d.). *Michigan State Government mentoring guidelines*. Available at http://www.michigan.gov/documents/Mentor_Guidelines_101422_7.pdf.

National Academy of Sciences, National Academy of Engineering and Institute of Medicine. (1997). *Adviser, teacher, role model, friend: On being a mentor to students in science and engineering*. Washington, DC: The National Academies Press. Available at https://www.nap.edu/read/5789/chapter/1.

National Center for O*NET Development. (2019). O*NET Career Exploration Tools. Washington, DC: US Department of Labor. Available at https://www.onetcenter.org/tools.html O*Net Interest Profiler.

Rhodes, J. (2011). Research corner: Ethical principles for youth mentoring relationships. MENTOR. National Mentoring Partnership: Alexandria, VA. Available at http://files.eric.ed.gov/fulltext/ED522075.pdf.

Schroer, W.J. (n.d.). Generations X, Y, Z and the others. *The Social Librarian*. Available at http://www.socialmarketing.org/newsletter/features/generation3.htm.

SREB. (2013, May). *Counseling for careers can connect students to a goal beyond high school graduation*. Newsletter of Best Practices from the 26th annual High Schools That Work Staff Development Conference, New Orleans, LA. Atlanta, GA: SREB. Available at https://www.sreb.org/sites/main/files/file-attachments/13v08w_bestpractices_counseling.pdf.

SREB. (2016, July 28). *Guidance and Strategies Needed to Jump-Start College and Careers*. Newsletter of Best Practices from the 29th annual High Schools That Work Staff Development Conference, Atlanta, GA. Atlanta, GA: SREB. Available at https://www.sreb.org/post/best-practices-2015-hstw-staff-development-conference.

chapter III
Developing a Support Network
Who's Got Your Back?

Your support system

These days, the question "Who's got your back?" sounds like part of a script from an action movie hero's dialogue, or maybe a line from a report on internet security! What's important to a teacher new to a CTE classroom, or even a seasoned veteran, is to remember that every teacher needs a support system. Not that we are setting ourselves up as self-help gurus or greeting card writers, but we really understand from experience the importance of building self-esteem. New CTE teachers, because of the environments that most work in, need to surround themselves with people who will build them up, even when it would be just as easy for people to tear them down.

So what does this support system look like? Well, we've taken our direction from Charles Darwin and developed a taxonomy of

CTE teacher supporters. Assuming that all of your CTE support team is human, and that all of the individuals in it come from the same "kingdom," we will jump to the category (or phyla, for you biology sticklers out there) of those who are "school-associated" and "non-school-associated." The non-school-associated category is composed mostly of two groups: family and friends. Though this group is always important, especially as a shoulder to cry on, we won't spend much time on it here. We are more concerned with the school-associated groups.

Within this category we have three basic subgroups: those who play a supervisory role, those who provide content expertise, and those who contribute instructional support. Those in a supervisory role may be responsible for evaluating your performance as a teacher. People like directors, principals, and supervisors generally fall into this category. Because this group provides instructional guidance and enforces school policy and operational procedures, this relationship is generally a bit formal. By that we mean that this relationship tends to be more of a "boss-to-employee" relationship, and the communication is generally directive. However, most CTE administrative leaders also form a more collaborative relationship when it comes to instructional strategies.

The second group consists of those who can provide content expertise. Most CTE teachers do not have the luxury of working with another teacher in the same content area, so typically this group consists of individuals from outside the school on technical or occupational advisory committees (OACs), also known as business or industry advisory boards, groups, or councils. These are individuals who represent the field from which the CTE teacher came. If you are teaching carpentry, these individuals might represent small- and large-scale contractors in your area, perhaps material suppliers, building code enforcement officials, or representatives of an association (like the state affiliate of the National Association of Home Builders). This group can help you find the pulse of your employer community and locate internships and cooperative education placements for your students. Most of all, this group will keep you up to date regarding new materials, processes, and equipment of which your students should be aware.

Our last group is probably the most important. This is the group of individuals who will help you find your balance. This group consists of peers, perhaps mentor teachers, instructional support communities, and professional associations. Life as a CTE professional is rewarding, but the general truth is that you are an army of one in most settings. Generally, no one in your building teaches the same content you do. That means usually no one is available with whom to share ideas or content-specific instructional strategies. If you are going to survive as a CTE professional, it is important that you build a network of support. This network will help you by serving as a sounding board for instructional ideas and a collaborative resource in developing long-range action plans. The bottom line is that it is good to know you are not alone in this new endeavor called CTE teaching. By interacting with those in these informal groups and networks, you will begin to develop some guidelines so you'll know if you are improving and having a positive effect on those smiling faces in your classroom.

Experiences from the field

No one likes solitary confinement, and no one likes working in an environment in which they don't receive frequent performance feedback. Fortunately, in our social media-connected world, developing a network has become a bit easier. Make sure you connect and stay connected to your new profession. Join national groups such as ACTE; they supply daily electronic briefings about CTE and have a LinkedIn group that may help you. Join statewide CTE associations in your field and attend as many professional development activities as you can. The trick is to never stop growing or learning about your new profession. Don't discount information published by other groups as well. These sorts of web pages, though typically theme focused, can provide valuable resources for individual teachers.

Also consider the valuable connections you gain from getting involved in the CTSO that serves your career cluster/technical area. Not only do students develop a great network, but you can also add to your professional network, work with other teachers, assist with competitive events, and attend professional development events.

In California, Regional Occupational Programs are one of the delivery systems for CTE in the state. Several years ago the Colton-Redlands-Yucaipa Regional Occupational Programs (CRY-ROP) was having difficulty retaining new CTE teachers. Feeling overwhelmed and under-supported, many of CRY-ROP's new teachers left the profession and went back to industry. Realizing the need to retain top industry talent in education, CRY-ROP developed a Teacher Induction Program (TIP). The TIP program started as a two-year induction program led by experienced teachers in the role of mentoring new CTE teachers and providing veterans with additional support. TIP program components include workshops and trainings, weekly communication between the mentor and teachers, and <u>non-evaluative</u> classroom visits and observations. After implementing the program, CRY-ROP's turnover rate decreased and classroom instruction improved significantly. CRY-ROP's TIP program earned a Model Program Award from the California Department of Education for this accomplishment.

The state of California also identified the need to support CTE teachers with professional development. Recognizing the success of CRY-ROP's TIP program, the California Department of Education funded and expanded the TIP model program statewide and renamed it CTE TEACH. CTE TEACH utilizes three strategies—an early online orientation program for new teachers, online professional development modules, and a teacher induction and mentoring program. The four cornerstones of CTE TEACH are to increase teacher retention, improve teacher training, enhance teacher effectiveness, and advance student learning. To date, CTE TEACH has trained over 200 mentors statewide who have provided direct support to over 500 new teachers. CTE TEACH professional development modules are a free resource that can be found at http://www.cteteach.cteonline.org.

The CTE TEACH program has had tremendous success in increasing teacher retention and effectiveness. State-trained mentors consistently report that new teachers are thriving, not just surviving. New teachers report that the assistance and support provided by mentors is key to their success. One of the most important components of mentoring is face time with the mentee. Often, new teachers come across a variety of situations unique to the teaching profession. Having a mentor available to listen and provide advice and feedback in a non-evaluative manner has proven to be critical to new teacher success. Simply put, a mentor is a "professional friend" who is there for the mentee.

The difference a mentor can make can be summed up with the following example. Four weeks into the school year, a new culinary arts teacher was hired directly from industry. She walked into a classroom that had been staffed by a substitute, had no lesson plans, and found the kitchen was a disaster! She was also expected to run the campus café, but none of her students were food-handler certified. Feeling the pressure, she turned to her mentor for support and guidance. The mentor was able to schedule meetings with the school principal and administrator to discuss a list of things that needed to happen in order for the café to begin serving. The mentor was also able to set up two shadowing days so that the new teacher could see how experienced culinary teachers on other campuses balanced classroom and kitchen management. The mentor also met with the mentee once a week to help her locate lesson plan ideas and plan the curriculum for the year.

This teacher reported that if it weren't for the mentor, she would have quit and gone back to work in industry. By the end of the school year, the teacher had built a portfolio of successful lesson plans, opened the café, and provided additional opportunities for her students to work on special-event catering and internships at local restaurants. Without a mentor as an additional resource, and without the opportunity to collaborate with other culinary instructors, this would not have been possible.

KEY POINTS FROM THIS CHAPTER

1. No man or woman is an island. Develop a support team!
2. Support can be formal or informal and can come from:
   a) friends and family
   b) supervisors
   c) members of Occupational Advisory Committees
   d) peers and mentors
3. Benchmark your success.
4. Never stop growing!
5. Stay connected professionally.
6. Find a mentor or professional friend!

RELATED CONTENT THAT MAY BE OF INTEREST

Carney, P., Crilley, E., Fala, J.T., Strouse, K., Tully, C., & Viviano, T. (2013). In-classroom coach: An addition to mentor teachers. *Techniques, (88)* 7, 50-55. Available at http://www.nxtbook.com/ygsreprints/ACTE/g36681_acte_techniques_oct2013/#/50.

Pawlowski, B. (2014). Backyard advocacy—How local business partners can help. *Techniques, (89)3, 34-37.*

Perna, M. (2006). Making the connection. *Techniques, (81)8*, 42-43. Available at https://eric.ed.gov/?q=Perna&ff1=dtySince_2000&ff2=aut Perna%2c+Mark+C.&id=EJ751462.

Schroer, D. (2014). Top five local advocacy tips for success. *Techniques, (89)3*, 38-41.

The National Coordinating Council for Career and Technical Student Organizations (NCC-CTSO). (2019). *Career Technical Student Organizations*. Available at http://www.ctsos.org/.

Handbooks:

Department of Career and Technical Education. (2019, March 6). *Program advisory committee guide*. Bismarck, ND: North Dakota Department of Education. Available at https://www.cte.nd.gov/sites/www/files/documents/Budget%20%26%20Finance/State-Carl%20 Perkins/AdvisoryCommitteeGuide.pdf. .

Michigan Department of Education. (2019, August). *Program advisory committee tool kit*. Lansing, MI: Office of Career and Technical Education. Available at https://www.michigan.gov/documents/mde/Program_Advisory_Tool_Kit_2017_597534_7.pdf.

chapter IV

Establishing a Positive Classroom Environment

To Form a More Perfect Union

Classroom culture

Maybe it was at your first junior high dance, or your first day at a new school, but all of us have felt out of place at some time in our lives. It's that feeling of being part of a group, but not really feeling like you belong, perhaps because you have no involvement in a group's operation. You may have even experienced that on a job site, as part of a community group, or even as a parent of a Little Leaguer. However, much research has been done to show that the need to belong is fundamental to human motivation. The environment of your classroom, and the culture, tone, and energy level have a huge impact on student success! You can visit classrooms and sense almost immediately when you talk to and observe students if they feel a sense of belonging—a feeling of being part of the effort. For both new and seasoned CTE teachers, it can be really fun and rewarding to develop your classroom environment to reflect a high-performance workplace, where collaborative and respectful partnerships exist, with a positive and productive vibe.

Part of the magic behind a positive classroom culture is the fundamental practice that all rules, procedures, practices, and expectations are built on respect. As teachers, we can use that wisdom to promote a respectful dynamic between and among students and adults. We can ask ourselves and our students, "What does it mean to be respected?" One key belief is that all students are valued for their contributions—although they have different talents, all students can make contributions. As you will learn in Chapter V: Establishing Student-Teacher Boundaries, it is difficult to value your students if you don't know them.

Another component of an effective and positive environment includes a system created for dealing with students who get off track or choose inappropriate actions. It is really difficult to deal with negative situations on the spot without having thought earlier of interventions and consequences—more on that topic in Chapter VIII.

Consider the long-lasting benefits of recognizing and celebrating student successes, from good attendance to a high-quality project outcome, to a polished written summary, to students choosing to help a peer with a challenging task. Think about how you can use the walls of your lab and classroom to communicate student success by displaying photos of students at work, posting their project results, challenging students to create technical displays, showcasing safety boards with information, and so forth. Even how you set up your classroom and lab space affects students' sense of belonging. Ask yourself if your students sit in a classroom configuration that suggests everyone belongs and can participate equally.

Just as you may have experienced being part of something, but may not have had true buy-in to the mission of the group, students can also experience this. As teachers, we can invite students to own much of their learning and success and feel the resulting deep sense of value by creating opportunities for students to participate and assist with classroom decisions. Work collaboratively to set goals for learning and define the level of quality and high expectations that students can achieve with commitment, perseverance, and focus. Discuss and model the value of effort;

for example, redoing work to meet high standards will ultimately bring intrinsic rewards. Figuring out that "sweet spot" of what is challenging and offering extra help can be a motivating combination and support student buy-in. Students have to feel that the goals and challenges are possible with effort.

Experiences from the field

As recommended in Chapter III, shifting some responsibility to students can be a win-win. Organize a classroom team structure whereby students assist in the operation of the day-to-day management of the classroom, much like in various industries. Students can take on roles, such as weekly supervisor, safety officer, or records manager, that help you as the teacher manage the learning while students are honing valuable workplace skills. Keep in mind that students may not have much experience in leadership or other roles, and they don't learn just by doing. They may need a little instruction, some guided practice, and resources on how to effectively enact their role(s). The West Virginia Department of Education (WVDE) has instituted a Simulated Workplace effort in CTE programs that puts the student at the forefront of the classroom by organizing it as a high-performance workplace. Resources for students can be found at: http://wvde. state.wv.us/simulated-workplace/.

A useful technique to help students to process lecture/theory information is Think-Pair-Share (http://www.readingquest.org/strat/tps.html). Also, it is helpful for students' engagement if you switch up instructional approaches (lecture, group discussion, hands-on activity, practice, etc.) approximately every 20 to 30 minutes. This keeps students' minds focused and helps them integrate new information. Invite students to partner or work in teams on lab-based projects (e.g., diagnosing an engine issue, preparing a storyboard, installing ductwork). Students can also collaborate when working on supporting knowledge/information tasks (e.g., calculating a bill of sale, determining the number of routers needed on a floor plan, understanding the stages of adolescent development). Providing students with opportunities to share ideas, complete complex tasks collaboratively, and team up around a challenge fuels positive energy in the classroom. See the resources for cooperative learning strategies.

Invite students to contribute their talents to improve the classroom and lab area; they can paint, create displays, work on a more efficient layout, and help with storage ideas and better ways to manage materials.

Get to know students through creative communication. Have your class write a creative group story that will be shared and include something fun about each classroom member (e.g., participated in a 5k, coaches a little league team, or raises goats on a family farm). Have students contribute personal words of wisdom about the week's learning challenges or current events that they share as reflective food-for-thought and discussion at the end of class.

Provide students with a way to measure their own effort each day for a week. This can be fun, but ensure you include criteria with a serious undertone. An automotive teacher could ask his or her students to reflect on their productivity and accomplishments toward their goals by asking, for example, "Were you burning rubber, just coasting, or backpedaling?" Have them summarize their measurements at the end of the week with a rationale about what influenced their productivity positively or not. Have a quick power meeting with each student to see if he/she was smokin' (burning rubber), breezin' (just coasting), or driftin' (backpedaling). Customize the categories/criteria for your CTE discipline.

Each year, a graphic arts teacher invites her students to create their own *South Park* character to express their individuality, not only to practice their design techniques, but also to become part of a classroom collection of characters. (*South Park* is an animated sitcom which is popular with millennial-aged students.) At graduation, this teacher provides each student with his/her own print of the classroom collection of characters for collecting signatures. These prints are coveted and valued by students! And, oh yes, the teacher's character is part of the group too!

Students in an agricultural class were challenged to create a class social contract that all the students signed and posted to show their commitment to a positive learning environment and to emphasize the need to support everyone in working toward their goals. This same agriculture class also developed a handbook, after researching what information was important and appropriate, that they adopted as their rules and protocols.

KEY POINTS FROM THIS CHAPTER

1. The environment of your classroom impacts student success.
2. Culture, tone, and energy level are critical.
3. Your classroom and lab must support a positive approach to learning.
4. Each student must feel, "I am worth the effort, and I can be successful!"
5. All classroom interactions must be based on mutual respect.
6. Involve students in decisions and create opportunities for students to work collaboratively, as in a high-performance workplace.

RELATED CONTENT THAT MAY BE OF INTEREST

Guido, M. (2017) Blog, The Guide to Cooperative Learning: Principles and Strategies for Each Type https://www.prodigygame.com/blog/cooperative-learning-principles-st

Wood, C., Porter, D., Brady, K. & Forton, M. (2003). Everyday rules that really work! *Instructor.* *113* (1), 25. http://www.scholastic.com/teachers/article/everyday-rules-really-work

chapter V
Establishing Student-Teacher Boundaries
Sometimes You Have to Build Fences

Relating to students

Being a teacher is like being a parent to other people's children, but 20 children at a time! As mentioned, these days a CTE teacher may spend more time with a student than his or her parents do. Research supports that teachers relating well to their students is one of the most significant factors in generating positive academic and social outcomes (Keddie, Amanda, and Churchill, Rick, 2005). For new CTE teachers who have children, have coached children, or who have taught children in other environments, establishing and enforcing student behavior in the school environment may be an easier task than for those who haven't had those experiences. Most people who decide to become CTE teachers do so because of their love of their craft and desire to help young people, at least in the experience of our authors! Do they hope that their students will respect them and come to regard them as important, influential adults? Most likely they do!

Setting boundaries

However, new teachers must remember that students are NOT to be treated as their peers. This concept is especially difficult for CTE teachers, because they have life experiences on shop floors, clinics, and labs. Their experiences in these environments dictate that employees work together towards common goals and targets, and age is rarely a factor. In a CTE environment, though, teachers must maintain authority and require a level of respect from their learners. This makes a CTE teacher's choice of language and interactions critical. Teachers are professionals charged with the task of guiding their students' growth and technical competence. Sometimes the content or competencies being delivered may not be fun or easy to achieve. This means that students will face challenges, and challenges usually stress relationships. A caring, supportive, motivating teacher is what students need to succeed, not a new best friend or peer.

CTE teachers are truly role models for students in actions, behaviors, and choices. Remember, though, there should be a line between being your students' teacher and being their peer. Whenever in doubt about that relationship, ask yourself, "Would I be comfortable sharing the action I'm about to take with my own family, friends, parents, and/or school administrators? Could this action become embarrassing or perhaps career-ending?"

Be especially careful concerning social media with regards to texting, readily available cell-phone cameras, Facebook, Twitter, Instagram, and so forth. Build "fences" to carefully separate your professional life regarding students from your personal life. Talk to other veteran educators, mentors, and administrators about any concerns you might have. Teachers' unions, trade associations, and some other professional organizations can provide advice and guidance concerning appropriate and inappropriate relationships between teachers and students, so don't be afraid to reach out. Bottom line: If it doesn't feel right, don't do it.

While keeping the relationship professional is critical, it is important for CTE teachers to develop opportunities to learn more about their students early on. Why did they enroll in their CTE program? What are their specific career interests? What do they like to do outside of school? These are all examples of questions to ask. Consider volunteering or chaperoning an activity that will allow you to see a different side of students than you see in class. You could help with a school fundraiser or some other school-wide activity, or perhaps do something with a CTSO. To create a healthy classroom environment, provide a stable emotional environment as well as one that provides instructional support; be sure to build in many opportunities for students to achieve success; and set up a climate of care, respect, and trust. Make sure that environment is consistent every day. Your classroom may be the most stable part of your learners' day.

Care • Respect • Trust

One of the simplest and most powerful things CTE teachers can do is to learn the names of their students as quickly as possible. When a teacher fails to call a student by name, the message to the student is that he or she is not worth the time it would take to learn his or her name. Take the class rosters and study the names, or use table tents the first week of class so that students will see you have an interest in connecting with them on an individual level. Since names tend to be a defining individual characteristic, learning names can help ease students' feeling of being just faces in a classroom. There is nothing sweeter for students to hear than the sound of their own name!

Experiences from the field

Getting to know your students on an individual level can seem to be a daunting task. One simple tool to speed this process up is to use a student survey, with questions such as:

1. Why did you become interested in the CTE program (engineering, automotive, health, etc.)?
2. Whom do you consider a mentor and why?
3. Where do you see yourself in five years?
4. Where do you see yourself in 10 years?
5. What interests/hobbies do you have outside of school?

With responses to these questions, you can gain needed insight about your students more quickly than by other means. You can periodically review these surveys with students to continue to refine future goals as they learn more in their chosen CTE area. The information can also be used with a student who is misbehaving by asking the student how the misbehavior is helping to reach his/her listed goals. Having individualized information about a student is a major asset in making a personal connection. It can be said that students don't care what you know until they know that you care!

You can extend the list of questions to initiate a goal-setting process, which is an important step toward careers for your students and further evidence of your commitment to work with them. Goal-setting questions might include the following:

1. Decide what you want to accomplish. What is your passion or desire?
2. When do you want to accomplish it?
3. What goal is believable to you?
4. Where are you now?
5. What obstacles do you need to overcome?
6. What knowledge do you need to acquire?
7. What does the employment opportunity look like for the near future? What are the potential salary ranges, work benefits, etc.?
8. What peers and/or groups should you associate with?
9. By developing an action plan, what one step can you take today? Write this down, prioritizing all the action steps. Take action!
10. Can you see yourself accomplishing the goal? Write a visualization statement in the present tense of that picture. Play the picture over and over in your mind. Read your visualization statement daily.
11. Decide never to quit until your goal is reached. Be persistent.

Teaching is a huge responsibility, but the benefits to the teacher are just as huge. When you hear former students explain that you have made a positive impact on their lives, you'll know how true that is!

Each teacher needs to develop a large toolbox of strategies that can be used with all types of students. Here are a few suggestions: Imagine each student is a website. Create an opportunity for a "10-second hit" in which you make contact with one student during each class. Some examples are:

- Make a comment about the student's appearance—new hairstyle, a cool T-shirt, unusual earrings, a different-colored nail polish, etc.
- Ask or comment about things that kids are doing outside of class—sports events, extracurricular activities, concerts, etc. Give students positive feedback about something they've done well in class recently.
- Check in tactfully with students who look tired or who are unusually quiet, upset, or rambunctious. Reflect back to them on what you see and give students a way to name what they've been feeling. You still need to refocus them quickly for class.
- When you are summarizing a discussion or linking ideas, mention students' names and comments they made earlier that contributed to a better understanding of the topic.

A new teacher took over for another teacher who left midyear. One student consistently stood back and watched his peers operate machinery rather than touch any himself. Consequently, that student was substantially behind in required project completions. The student had an IEP, so some modifications in the shop were expected, but certainly the IEP didn't allow for not completing projects. The previous teacher had given this student high grades. The new CTE teacher decided to get to know this student right away, give him step-by-step guidance on a machine, and provide positive verbal reinforcement as he progressed.

At first the student asked the teacher why he wasn't yelling at him all of the time like his father did, or why he didn't just leave him alone like the former teacher did. The new teacher responded that his expectations for classwork and project completion were the same for all of his students. There's that consistency again! The new CTE teacher recognized that this one student needed additional guidance, patience, and support. The new teacher also reached out to the classroom aide and parents in a professional, positive way in hopes of gaining their support for this student as well.

Gradually, the student began operating machinery. Although it took him longer to complete projects, he was building confidence in operating the machinery and gaining more skills than were previously expected of him. The new teacher recognized early that he needed to establish a positive relationship with this student and it paid off.

KEY POINTS FROM THIS CHAPTER

1. Establishing mutual respect between the teacher and student is critical.
2. Students should not be treated as your peers.
3. You are the role model!
4. Think before posting anything on social media.
5. Be a motivating, caring, supportive education professional.

RELATED CONTENT THAT MAY BE OF INTEREST

Chen, D. & McGeehan, P. (2012, May 1). Social media rules limit student-teacher contact. *The New York Times*, p.20. Available at https://www.nytimes.com/2012/05/02/nyregion/social-media-rules-for-nyc-school-staff-limits-contact-with-students.html.

Faculty Development and Instructional Design Center. (2015.). A Tutorial on Faculty Student Relationships: Balancing Roles and Maintaining Boundaries. DeKalb, Il: Northern Illinois University College of Education. Available at https://www.niu.edu/facdev/resources/relationships/presentation.html.

Fritsch, J. M. (2014). Beyond the workshop. *Techniques, (89)*5, 16-19. Available at https://www.acteonline.org/publications/techniques/techniques-archives/.

National Association of State Directors of Teacher Education and Certification. (2015). Model Code of Ethics for Educators (MCEE). Washington, DC: NASDTEC. Available at https://www.nasdtec.net/page/MCEE_Doc.

chapter VI
Setting Behavior and Learning Expectations
What Do You Need From Me?

Expectations

You may have faced a new classroom full of students and felt a moment of panic. The truth is that the first time you meet a new class is the right time to start forming the relationship that will determine many of your successes or failures as a new CTE teacher. No matter what performance targets are set or standards adopted for the curriculum, the teacher in the classroom is the one element that makes the biggest difference for each student. Teachers have to plan and generate experiences so that students build on their initial interest in the technical field they have selected. They have elected to enroll in your CTE program, but they need you to be the catalyst to make them want to stay. From the very first day of class, build into every lesson a compelling reason to learn. You were hired as an expert in your field, so share your experience—that's what students want to see and hear about! This sharing makes lessons relevant and helps build a commitment to learning.

In planning for that first day and week of school, create situations that engage students. CTE teachers must share their expectations for appropriate student behavior, what materials are to be brought to the classroom each day, homework completion, and preparedness for quizzes and tests, but it shouldn't all be crammed into that first day. As mentioned in Chapters IV and V, it may be more important to get to know students and to help students get to know each other. As James Comer states, "In real estate it is location, location, location. In education it is relationships, relationships, relationships." He further states, "No significant learning occurs without a significant relationship." (Payne, 2008). Often in CTE environments, students come from several sending schools and may know only a few other students. They may feel apprehensive about being around so many new people and new expectations. Begin to build new positive relationships through some small-group activities that will allow students to share in a positive way.

So, what are the basics concerning expectations that a teacher should consider working in to the early days of class? Student behavior is a big one. What should students be expected to do as they enter the classroom each day? Should they bring certain clothes with them? And how long should they take in the locker area to change into these clothes? When are they permitted to leave the shop, lab, or classroom? What materials (notebook, pencil, text, tools, calculators, etc.) are expected each day? How will the instructor signal when he or she is ready to begin class? And don't forget expectations related to new technology; many schools have an "Acceptable Use" policy which covers use of computers, browsers, and cell phones in the classroom.

Another area for decisions regarding behavior is about when and how a student can ask questions, as well as options for answering them. There are a multitude of options! Will it be by always raising a hand first? Will students submit questions on a mobile whiteboard? Will they ask questions through a ticket-out-the-door format? How about answering questions? Will they answer some short-response questions as a group (choral response)? Will they sometimes use individual student response boards (whiteboards with markers or electronic response systems)? Will there be cooperative learning/collaborative opportunities (group projects, Think-Pair-Share review activities)? Will there be times when students may make choices for some of their learning, thus giving them more input and empowerment in a positive way?

Once established, maintaining ground rules and expectations for appropriate behavior will be important too. A mentor or administrator can be very helpful here. Remember that what might work well for one person might not work well for another. Just as parents have different parenting styles, not all teachers will have the same rules/styles, and this can sometimes become confusing to students. Develop classroom and shop rules that are simple, safe, fair, and consistent, and don't slack off just because a holiday is around the corner or it is almost the end of the school year. Think about creating an opportunity for students to exercise leadership skills by working through a process to determine a set of norms to live by in their class/lab. Challenge them to set up a learning environment that reflects a modern workplace. Refer to the "Related content that may be of interest" section at the end of this chapter for a process to set workplace/ team norms. New CTE teachers can be especially hard on themselves when things don't seem to go as planned, but even veteran teachers can have occasional bad days. Stick to your guns. With thoughtful planning, much patience, and persistence, most of your days will be good ones.

In the next two sections you will notice that there are examples which appear to be duplicative of other ideas you have seen in this book. You might see ideas about icebreakers, which could fall in the category of getting to know your students, but in this context they serve to help you understand what things interest your students and keep them focused. Bell-ringer activities have a similar function; they provide focus. When students are focused on learning something to which they can relate, they are more likely to stay on task and follow your expectations. It's brilliant; you get two benefits for one activity!

Experiences from the field

Teachers have suggested a variety of small-group activities that can act as icebreakers. One is a questionnaire about students which they can complete and exchange with other students as a way to introduce each other in an informal and possibly fun manner. A variation on the questionnaire is to give each student a sheet that has three columns and a place for three students' names. Then ask students to pair up with someone they don't know well or use grouping cards to place them. Give each pair two minutes to write down in one column all the similarities they can think of, physical attributes, interests, family things, possessions they own, and so forth. Ask students to pair up two more times. Once all the parings have been completed, ask, "What surprised you about what you found you had in common?" "How many similarities did you find the first time?" Point out that when we are having a disagreement or having trouble working together, it's especially important to remember what we have in common.

Another student interaction activity could be a bingo card with hobbies, sports, music groups, etc., on which students ask classmates to sign the spaces labeled with what they like. It could be a puzzle with a variety of major topics about your subject area that students put together, maybe with some sort of an incentive for completion. One teacher's first-day activity was to appear in front of the class as a rapper, complete with clothing and jewelry typically worn by a rap star. The teacher proceeded to rap to music with rewritten lyrics to describe some of the topics that would be taught that year. At first students were stunned, but after the teacher's solo, they broke out into applause. Students in that teacher's class certainly didn't tell their parents that their teachers had all done the same boring first-day stuff!

ICE BREAKERS

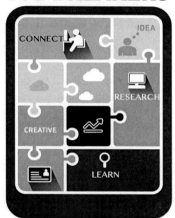

Some teachers utilize a bell ringer to focus their students when it is time to begin a lesson. One way is to make a statement such as, "May I have your attention now?" Other teachers flicker the classroom lights briefly or count down from five fingers to one to signal

IN ACTION!

that it is time to stop socializing and focus on what the teacher will do next. Sometimes a teacher will show a cartoon related to the day's lesson, or post a picture of a new tool or piece of equipment to begin to gauge what his or her students do or do not know about it. This teaching strategy using focus and engagement of students from the beginning of the lesson is called an activation strategy, and there is much research on the topic; go ahead and Google it.

A strategy utilized by a number of teacher preparation programs around the country is to sit with your mentor or another experienced teacher to prepare before the school year begins. If possible, concentrate on mapping out the first few weeks of school. Week one will probably deal with orientation and safety, week two might be how to pull dents on a damaged car, or another task from your curriculum. Remember that an effective teacher strives for a good mix of classroom instruction and real-world application of that information.

Arrange with your administrator to observe experienced, successful, well-established teachers. If you cannot find one in your subject area, it doesn't matter. You are really looking for the best strategies in this case, not teaching content. Pay particular attention to how successful teachers handle routine classroom procedures (e.g., locker area procedure, notebook/textbook placed on desk, students copying the essential question).

Consider writing a one-page letter to be mailed or emailed to the families of your students. Choose two or three things you want them to know about you and your course:

- Describe your course, including requirements, goals, and key learnings.
- Describe your hopes and expectations for students.
- Share what might be challenging for students in this class. Be concise and positive in presenting those lessons or skills, and maintain a sense of humor despite hearing some sighing and moaning at times.
- Let parents know what steps they can take if students are having trouble meeting class requirements.
- Let parents know they are welcome to communicate with you and share the best times and ways to contact you.
- Emphasize that effort, attitude, and participation really count in your classroom. Identify some of the social, academic, and technical skills you hope students will learn during the year.

Also consider making good-news calls or sending emails to compliment a student's participation, progress, citizenship, or other class contribution. Parents appreciate contact that isn't always disciplinary or improvement related.

Some teachers create interview sheets and then ask students to find a partner and choose a question that interests them both. They should write down basic information to introduce their partner to the rest of the class. Here are some of the questions used:

- What's one place you would like to visit in your lifetime? Why?
- What is your favorite TV show and why do you like to watch it?
- If you had to eat the same meal every day for a month, what would it be?
- What's one thing that you would like to change in your neighborhood that would make it a better place to live?
- What worries you most about the world you live in today?
- Name one thing you could teach another person to do or make.
- What's your favorite holiday of the year? What makes this day special?
- What's one thing that you would like to change about your school that would make it a better place for you?

A veteran teacher learned an efficient way to provide his students with a way to gain his attention whenever he was involved with another student. He gave students a sheet of paper inside a sheet protector that had a smiley face that stated, "Please help me." Whenever a student had a question or needed help in the shop area and the teacher was already involved with another student, the student needing help simply handed the "Please help me" sheet to the instructor and returned to his or her workstation. When the teacher completed helping one student, he knew which student he was to help next. The reminder served to help students establish an orderly way to request help in a noisy environment while maintaining respect for fellow students.

We know a teacher who works in a CTE secondary program whom we'll refer to as Mr. G, as his students refer to him. Mr. G greets students at the door and welcomes them to the classroom each day by shaking hands with each student, modeling a good firm handshake and eye contact. The students sit in a circle at the beginning of class as a way to acknowledge that they are a community of learners who are in this together, not just individuals competing with one another, rushing in, doing their time, and scrambling out when the bell rings. He always has an opening activity for class that gathers all the students into a group to establish cohesiveness and to check the overall mood.

Mr. G makes personal connections with each student throughout the class period. He also shares something about his life with students, inviting students to consider his classroom as a place where people can feel safe to be real instead of going through the motions of being someone others want them to be. This creative CTE teacher also generates opportunities for students to construct major projects around something that matters to them. Each year students create an action research project that links the local community to their interests and the content. He strives to make this content more meaningful by personalizing the learning for each student's goals and interests. The end of Mr. G's class is marked by a closing activity to reflect on what was learned in the class and to help establish direction for the next time the class meets.

KEY POINTS FROM THIS CHAPTER

1. Don't cram every student expectation into the first day.
2. Get to know your students and help them know each other.
3. Relationships are critical to learning.
4. Build a sense of fairness and consistency.
5. Establish a long-term plan and share it.

RELATED CONTENT THAT MAY BE OF INTEREST

Bottoms, G. & Phillips, I. (2010). *Skills for a lifetime: Teaching students the habits of success*. Atlanta, GA: Southern Regional Education Board. Available at https://www.sreb.org/sites/main/files/file-attachments/10v25_skills_for_a_lifetime_intro.pdf.

Lieber, C. M. (2009). *Getting classroom management right: Guided discipline and personalized support in secondary schools*. Cambridge, MA: Educators for Social Responsibility. Accessed September 9, 2019 at https://positiveclassroomrelationships.weebly.com/worksheets.html.

Massachusetts Department of Education. (2008). *A toolkit for new teachers*. Lexington, MA: Minuteman Regional Vocational Technical School District. Available at http://www.tantasqua.org/superintendent/teachingandlearning/docs/helpfullinks/NewTeacherToolkit2008.pdf.

Payne, R. (2008). Nine powerful practices. *Educational Leadership, 65*(7), 48-52. Available at http://www.ascd.org/publications/educational-leadership/apr08/vol65/num07/Nine-Powerful-Practices.aspx.

Rice, C. (2012). *Creative strategies for CTE teachers* (NC CTE Comprehensive Support Model). Available at http://scotlandcte.files.wordpress.com/2012/08/creative-strategies-handbook.pdf.

Terada, Y. (2019, August 7). 8 Proactive Classroom Management Tips. Lucas Education Research. Available at https://www.edutopia.org/article/8-proactive-classroom-management-tips.

The Learning System. (2013, Summer). Creating Norms. Oxford, OH: Learning Forward. Available at https://learningforward.org/docs/default-source/learning-system/ls-sum13-creating-norms-tool.pdf.

Westerberg, T. (2013, September 17). *Instructional leadership: Walking the talk*. InService Blog. Alexandria, VA: ASCD Available at http://inservice.ascd.org/books/instructional-leadership-walking-the-talk/.

chapter VII
Organizing a Safe Lab Environment
A Place for Everything

Workshop area safety concerns

Lathes, vertical mills, hydraulic lifts, lions, tigers, and bears—oh my! So many machines, tools, and pieces of equipment are needed in the work area, and all of them involve potential dangers and hazards that could cause injury or be life-threatening. The teacher must be able to supervise ALL students in that vast area, pretty much at the same time. Unless the teacher is some type of towering alien octopus-type creature with multiple eyes and appendages, this can certainly be a challenge. From observing students and identifying safety concerns, to demonstrating how to turn the myriad controls at each machine, to answering the endless questions asked by students over a two- to three-hour period, a CTE teacher may feel a bit overwhelmed. Let's think about some simple rules that should be put into place from day one for our students' (and our own) safety.

First and foremost, every person in the shop/lab area must know the location of the main power supply, as well as the individual machine on/off switches, emergency shutoffs, etc. A discussion with students should center on situations that might lead up to the use of some of these features in the event of an emergency.

Prior to each student beginning to use a particular piece of equipment, the teacher should provide a handout for the machine's main features (e.g., a diagram identifying the main machine parts), safety guidelines and concerns, and a list of simple dos and don'ts. A new CTE teacher may be able to borrow this from another teacher or mentor. If not, a lot of this information is in the paperwork and manufacturer's manual that accompanies each piece of machinery; or it may be found online and can be easily adapted for student safety sheets.

The teacher should give a demonstration of the correct operation of each machine as he/she discusses the information provided on the student's safety sheet. Next, one or two student volunteers should demonstrate safe operation while answering related questions. Finally, each student should sign and date the safety sheet for each machine before being permitted to operate it. Signed safety sheets should be placed in students' files and the students should retain a copy for their ongoing reference. This is not only for everyone's personal safety but can also help protect the teacher from a liability standpoint, in the event of an accident that occurs under his or her supervision.

Other safety activities are to have students identify the location of fire extinguishers and fire blankets; showers or eyewash stations (for chemical burns); chemicals in metal storage cabinets; spill cleanup materials and procedures; air and gas shutoffs; electrical panels first aid kits; SDS (Safety Data Sheets); and so forth. (US Consumer Safety Product Commission, 2006).

Work areas and machine stations can quickly become cluttered and messy, posing potential safety hazards. This is true whether you are a welding teacher, business teacher, or marketing teacher and it is extremely important to require students to clean up their work area at the end of every class period. For too many students, this is just not a fun thing to do at the end of every day. (Should we take a look at their bedrooms to see how organized and clean they are at home? Ah, probably not, unless we want to have nightmares!) The teacher should insist on each student doing his or her part in cleaning up the shop/lab at the end of every day. One or two students could be assigned as safety supervisors to oversee cleanup if the teacher wants to free up time for other end-of-the-day routines.

All machines, equipment, and instruments should be properly cleaned and shut down; tools returned to storage sites; waste materials properly disposed of; items restocked; and broken tools reported to the teacher and/or replaced. By doing this, students will get into a routine of safety and cleanliness appropriate to the workplace. Students can learn a process from the lean manufacturing field called 5S (or 6S if you include safety). Students can use the 5S process to overhaul their work areas. Refer to the "Related content that may be of interest" section at the end of this chapter for more information about this. A clean shop is a happy shop—and a safer one too!

The new CTE teacher also needs to know other basics for the work environment if an accident were to occur: 1) the policies and procedures for basic first aid, 2) the most direct way to contact the school nurse, and 3) how these kinds of incidents should be reported to the administration.

One more critical step in setting up and establishing a safe work environment is communicating to students that there is NO room or tolerance for horseplay! The teacher should clarify expectations of proper student behavior, both in the classroom and live-work areas. You'll find more information on student behavior in Chapter VII: Setting Behavior and Learning Expectations and Chapter VIII: Creating Instructional Plans. Both of these chapters talk about ways to prepare students to receive information in a classroom, shop, lab, or clinic setting. Students need to understand what is and is not acceptable concerning their behavior both individually and toward classmates.

Often a teacher will provide a separate handout about behavior expectations and consequences. These handouts should be discussed, signed by the students, and placed in students' personal files. A caution is not to create too many rules. The KIS phrase, "Keep It Simple," works well in developing ground rules for behavior that are easy for students to understand and for the teacher to implement. One of our authors recalls a story that students talked about each year; an English teacher explained that most of society's rules really boil down to this phrase: "Be nice." Being respectful of others' property means being nice. Not calling people names or performing negative actions is being nice. That really might be the key safety rule!

For a new CTE teacher without prior teaching experience, who comes directly from a different profession into education, it can be a challenge to monitor students' safety in the shop or lab while teaching another group of students in the classroom. That mythical creature of many eyes who was mentioned earlier returns to mind. Think about the example of a new precision machine technology teacher delivering his first lesson to a section of students in the classroom. He is so focused on using his newly created PowerPoint presentation and student-guided note sheet that he doesn't think to look periodically into the live-work area to monitor what the remainder of the students are doing. This teacher needs to understand the importance of keeping a watchful eye on the students, no matter their location. Are they on task? Are they following safety procedures? Is their behavior appropriate?

Having multiple, swiveling eyes may not be an option for humans, but sometimes we must learn to watch students located in a variety of learning environments at the same time. The reality, though, is that a CTE teacher should never have students working in a lab environment unsupervised. No one ever wants to learn that a student was injured on his or her watch and that it could have been prevented by more vigilance. The good news is that a teacher's sixth sense does improve with time and experience.

Experiences from the field

One entertaining way to share this vital information with students is to set up a "shop scavenger hunt" with students competing individually or in teams to find safety-related switches, equipment, or safety concerns. Safety should always be an ongoing concern, so the teacher might appoint a different student to oversee general shop safety each week.

One of the more time-consuming tasks for a new CTE teacher may be "policing" students in the lab area to ensure they are all following the established safety rules. Wearing safety glasses within most programs is a very basic rule, but one which requires a great deal of monitoring. Some teachers are able to shift part of this responsibility to the students themselves, instead of having teachers be the constant reminder of safety-glasses usage. Depending on your environment and student level, one way to accomplish this is to have students take ownership of this rule. For example, one teacher presented the students with this problem in an effort to find a solution that would benefit everyone, and students came up with a viable solution that worked year after year. Their solution was that if Student A caught Student B without safety glasses in the lab area, Student B had to buy Student A a beverage (iced tea, water, soda, etc.) at break time.

As you can imagine, students policed each other after this consequence was applied, which gave the teacher more time to concentrate on his teaching role; very rarely did this teacher have to remind someone about wearing safety glasses. But be careful: even good solutions can have consequences! One day the teacher walked out of his office into the lab area with his own safety glasses more on top of his head than covering his eyes and was busted by a student. Rules are for everyone, and the teacher had no problem buying this student a beverage at break time!

A manufacturing teacher inherited a classroom and lab that was not physically conducive for students to team up, for the instructor to move about, or for safe access to the equipment. To create a sense of ownership and to show students how industries may organize/lay out a production floor, he challenged students to redesign the lab area; determine and create all the needed safety signage; and paint the floors to designate machine locations, workflow, and safety zones. When anyone visits this classroom now, a student is asked to give a tour and explain the redesign.

An excellent online resource about monitoring student behavior and setting up a safe shop environment is the Massachusetts Department of Education's *A Toolkit for New Teachers* (2008). It states the following: "Be on your feet with your eyes on students all of the time. Move about the room. Listen to everything being said. Let students know that you are always paying attention to what they are doing. Using a clipboard is very helpful when monitoring student work in a shop or lab setting." Additional information is provided for organizing the shop for safety, developing a shop floor-plan layout, and developing a student safety training log.

KEY POINTS FROM THIS CHAPTER

1. Safety starts the first day!
2. Help students to become familiar with the location of safety equipment and the procedures for its use.
3. KIS: Develop a short, simple list of rules and implement and enforce it.
4. Seek help; ask peers, mentors, and administrators to share and give feedback.
5. Be nice. (You'll have to read the chapter for the reference.)

RELATED CONTENT THAT MAY BE OF INTEREST

Massachusetts Department of Education. (2008). *A toolkit for new teachers*. Lexington, MA: Minuteman Regional Vocational Technical School District. Available at http://www.tantasqua.org/superintendent/teachingandlearning/docs/helpfullinks/NewTeacherToolkit2008.pdf.

NIOSH. (2003). *Safety checklist program for schools*. DHHS (NIOSH) Publication Number 2004-101. Washington, DC: Author. Available at http://www.cdc.gov/niosh/docs/2004-101/resources.html.

OSHA. (2011). Laboratory Safety Electrical Hazards. OSHA Quick Facts. Washington, DC: Occupational Safety and Health Administration. Available at https://www.osha.gov/Publications/laboratory/OSHAquickfacts-lab-safety-electrical-hazards.pdf.

OSHA newsletter subscription: Available at https://www.osha.gov/as/opa/quicktakes/qtpostcard.html.

Pace University (2014, August). *Wood & Finishing Shop Safety Plan*. NY, NY: PACE University Environmental Health and Safety. Available at https://www.pace.edu/sites/default/files/files/wood-finishing-shop-safety-plan.pdf.

Safety Culture. (2019). Safety Culture: 5S Plus Safety. St Louis MO: Safety Culture. Available at https://safetyculture.com/topics/6s-lean/.

US Consumer Safety Product Commission. (2006). *School Chemistry Laboratory Safety Guide*. Washington, DC: Department of Health and Human Services. Available at www.cdc.gov/niosh/docs/2007-107/pdfs/2007-107.pdf.

Zirkle, C. (2013). Don't let legal issues put you in hot water! A safety and liability primer. *Tech Directions, 72*(6) 17-23. Available at http://www.omagdigital.com/publication/?i=139140.

chapter VIII
Creating Instructional Plans
Don't Paint in the Dark

Planning with a purpose

Learning happens at any time, in any place, and is a constant in our lives. When you are building a garage or hosting a dinner, every moment and decision is filled with learning new techniques, reaffirming what you know works, or redoing steps because of change. So, it may seem strange as a new teacher to be asked to develop plans to represent what your students will learn versus "going with the flow" of everyday life. You may have heard, or even experienced, the wisdom of the old saying, "You can help to achieve your goals by writing them down." There is truth to this saying, and it is one good reason that planning what students can and will accomplish supports growth and achievement.

If you believe that an important function of CTE teaching is keeping track of what students learn, then planning your course of action is a necessity. Why? One of the most important reasons that teachers are asked to plan their lessons and projects is that you cannot measure what you don't define. Eight to ten key skills may be involved in moving a patient to/from a hospital bed, but if you don't plan how to best teach, practice, and evaluate these skills, how can you answer the BIG question of, "Do students get it?"

Just as builders use blueprints for structures, effective CTE teachers create large-scale and small-scale plans for instruction. Not only do students learn and develop technical skills while working with you, but they also gain academic and 21st century workplace readiness skills. These three domains of knowledge and skills—technical, academic, and workplace readiness—make up career readiness, as defined by ACTE. CTSOs are especially valuable for teaching foundational skills, such as teamwork and leadership, which are so important to a student's long-term success. (Find out more about these skills at Partnership for 21st Century Skills: http://www.p21.org/our-work/p21-framework.) Planning tools common to educators help to "map out" what you will teach and how you will assess student learning. One such tool available from SREB, *Planning for Improved Student Achievement*, helps teachers write standards-based units of study and plan their class periods.

Let's start from a large-scale view and move to a small-scale view. A curriculum map acts as a calendar to chart the timing of what you will teach for a year and a course syllabus communicates the nuts and bolts of a course, by semester or month or even week. A unit plan addresses learning goals and activities for a week or more, so it can be used as a project plan. On the smallest scale, the lesson plan acts as your game plan for a class period—what is expected of students, how you will kick off the day, the flow of activities, and so forth. Lessons should have an objective, which is what you wish the outcome of the lesson to be, and that should support your big questions. Think of your objective beginning with, "At the end of our time together today, students will be able to ..."

You will want to visit with your director/leader to learn what plans are required or mandated and if there are specific templates to use or guidelines to follow.

When considering important aspects of a lesson plan and how you can structure a lesson with a cyclic nature, it may also be helpful to think of the "Five E's": engage, explore, explain, elaborate, and evaluate. (Bybee, Crissman, Heil, Kuerbis, Matsumoto, & McInerney, 1989).

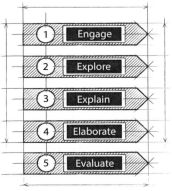

Start with *engage*–a technique to hook students' attention into the purpose of the day. Then invite students to *explore* the focus of the lesson to learn it, such as trying to develop questions using provided materials. As the teacher and students work through questions and feedback, students *explain* their understanding of the process. Students extend their thinking, practice, and *elaborate* by applying their new learning to other contexts. Lastly, students and teachers assess the learning and the lesson—this E of *evaluate* informs the next E of engage ... hence the cycle! See a description of this cycle at: https://nasaeclips.arc.nasa.gov/teachertoolbox/the5e#collapseOne

Experiences from the field

Lesson planning is your way of constantly reacting to what your students are or are not learning. All lessons, projects, activities, evaluations, and time spent should be driven by BIG questions—those questions essential to your course goals. Teachers who have gotten on a planning "roll" tend to identify the big questions of their course and their units and use those as guideposts for all of their planning. Keeping your lesson plans and other planning documents in some organized place, whether a file cabinet or an online storage source such as live binders or Google Docs, makes it easier to refer to what you did and when you did it and gives you a road map for instruction. It can also be really helpful to develop a habit of making quick notes after a lesson is completed on what worked well and what didn't go as planned. Your students can be a great source of feedback for how to improve a lesson. Give them an exit slip or ticket-out-the-door assignment to write down one thing they liked about the lesson and one thing they might do differently. Ask them to submit that to you as they leave for the day.

A technique to help you keep your focus while in the midst of a lesson is to prepare a list of some key questions ahead of time. Use an index card and capture two or three good questions that will challenge students. Carry that index card with you throughout the lesson so that you can refer to it and remember to ask those questions. Teachers also have found real value in posting the big questions of the unit/lesson in large print in a visible place so they can keep revisiting the questions and checking in with students as they know more and can give answers.

Visuals are a big part of the graphic design world. Use of visuals can also be a helpful strategy when tracking student learning and keeping lessons and activities planned and running smoothly. A graphics art teacher we know uses rolling whiteboards to display the big questions of his projects/lessons and the agreed-upon timelines—all posted in a fun way for student (and teacher) reference. For example, his students may be in the proofing phase of their project, so each day he updates the calendar with where they are in the process and how much time is remaining, e.g., four out of five proofing days left! This models great time/project management and complements his lesson timing.

Teachers in a school in Georgia plan lessons using three organizers: "I do" (modeling), "We do" (guided practice), and "You do" (independent practice and application). For modeling, the teachers may introduce the lesson with a vocabulary activity such as a word sort, or a teacher may demonstrate a technique such as using knives in culinary classes. Guided practice may still be teacher-led, but provides students with opportunities to practice the skills, often through cooperative learning activities, while teachers check for understanding through observation. Students can supplement what teachers observe by signaling their understanding using red or green cards, thumbs up/thumbs down, or with a number (one to four) that indicates their level of understanding. Independent practice and application is focused on allowing students to individually develop the skill or strategy further through repetition.

Most school systems evaluate teachers using rubrics for classroom observations, and evidence of planning is a key rubric component. You might review your lesson plans using some of these questions: Did I target specific district/state standards? Is something included to hook the attention and interest of students? Are there questions and activities that reflect higher-order thinking? Are the instructional activities well sequenced? Is there a clear closing activity that demonstrates students' understanding and sets up the next day's instruction? A health sciences teacher calls upon a student randomly at the end of every class to address the essential question for the day.

Social media can be used creatively to engage students and leverage their interest in smart phones or other technology-based methods of communication. A teacher in Wisconsin has set up text-message reminders of important dates and key learning objectives, which can also be shared on the school's Facebook site or general email accounts. The key is to use several methods to engage students in an active learning moment. Another example that works is to engage students in active teaching, whereby a student is assigned the responsibility of informing the other students of key objectives and deadlines. Rather than writing assignments on the whiteboard, ask a student to conduct a verbal check at the beginning of the class at selected points throughout the unit or course to reaffirm that information has been shared successfully. Sometimes just hearing directions from another peer/student makes all the difference. Another benefit of using this student-to student communication is that it helps to develop leadership skills.

Videos are always engaging. You might develop a series of fun and creative video links that effectively convey the content, along with tips to entice students to watch the videos. Another CTE teacher has each student or group of students produce a one-minute YouTube video on their final projects. The teacher selects one video that includes key objectives and learning outcomes that the students need to understand and posts it for the next class. Students like it because their work is recognized, and they can be creative with the project assignments. Teachers like it because it is another way to verify that content is being mastered, yet it can also serve as a creative way to market student success and engagement.

KEY POINTS FROM THIS CHAPTER

1. Teaching without planning is like painting in the dark.
2. Pay attention to the results of a lesson.
3. Ask students what happened each day to help inform the next lesson.
4. Lesson plans are unique to students and subjects.
5. Remember the Five E's when planning a lesson. (You'll have to read the chapter for these.)
6. Have students "experience" the learning.

RELATED CONTENT THAT MAY BE OF INTEREST

Bybee, R.W., Buchwald, C. E., Crissman, S., Heil, D. R., Kuerbis, P. J., Matsumoto, C., & McInerney, J. D. (1989). *Science and technology education for the elementary years: Frameworks for curriculum and instruction*. Washington, D.C.: Office of Educational Research and Improvement (ED). Available at https://eric.ed.gov/?id=ED314237.

Carr, J. & Bertrando, S. (2012). Top 10 instructional strategies for struggling students. *Leadership, 42* (1), 24-26, 38. Available at http://eric.ed.gov/?id=EJ983557.

Danielson, C. (2008). *The handbook for enhancing professional practice*. Alexandria, VA: ASCD.

Fink, J. L. W. (2014). No-sweat lesson prep. *Instructor, 123*(5), 45-47. Available at http:// https://www.scholastic.com/teachers/articles/teaching-content/no-sweat-lesson-prep/.

Hake, K. (2009). Career Activities and Vocational Lesson Plans. Vocational Information Center. Available at http://www.khake.com/page94.html.

Harbin, B. & Bottoms, G. (2008). *Planning for improved student achievement*. Atlanta, GA: Southern Regional Education Board. Available at https://www.sreb.org/sites/main/files/file-attachments/08v05_sbu_intro.pdf.

Kosloski, M. (2014, February). Making CTE work through CTSOs. *Techniques, 89*(2), 34-37. Available at http://www.nxtbook.com/ygsreprints/ACTE/g39344_acte_feb2014/index.php?startid=34.

NASA. (n.d.). The 5E instructional model. NASA eClips. Available at https://nasaeclips.arc.nasa.gov/teachertoolbox/the5e#collapseOne.

Partnership for 21st Century Learning. (2019). Framework for 21st Century Learning. Columbus, OH: Battelle for Kids. Available at http://static.battelleforkids.org/documents/p21/P21_Framework_Brief.pdf.

Saavedra, A.R. & Opfer, D. V. (2012, October 24). Nine lessons on how to teach 21st century skills. *Education Week, (32)* 9. Available at http://www.rand.org/blog/2012/10/nine-lessons-on-how-to-teach-21st-century-skills-and.html.

chapter IX
Challenging Students and Providing Feedback

Thrill of Victory or Agony of Defeat!

Challenging students

Do you ever wonder why, when observing a group of teenagers or adults, maybe on an athletic field organizing a pick-up game of Ultimate Frisbee, some of the players will jump right in, "no-holds-barred," and others will sit back a bit and watch and wait for the moment when they will engage in the task? You may see this difference among students in the classroom; some are ready to take on the challenge and others may be more hesitant. Of central importance for any teacher is how to challenge students, and it is an undertaking with many perspectives to consider: Do students think they can achieve the goal? Is it interesting or worthy of their effort? Do students know they can access help and that it is okay to fail?

Abraham Maslow, a psychologist who studied human needs (www.simplypsychology.org/maslow.html), suggested all humans have a need for achievement and a need to realize their full potential. In order for us to tap into these needs in our students, we must cultivate an atmosphere of high expectations *and* support, in which students will feel safe in challenging themselves. Teachers are in a powerful position to foster their students' beliefs that they can achieve. Meeting with students regularly to help them set and monitor goals can keep them striving—and help them to see their progress!

Another must-have in terms of challenging students is frequent and specific feedback. Feedback is a powerful means to motivate students to achieve. The feedback that is most helpful for student learning includes *specific information* about what they have done correctly and what they need to rethink. It is best to provide feedback soon after students attempt something so they can ponder it while their efforts are fresh in their mind. It can also be a great motivator to invite students to reflect on the level of their achievement and determine their own feedback. Feedback should also reflect the criteria you are striving to meet in the assignment or project. For example, students participating in a local/classroom CTSO competition will improve much more when feedback is provided using the contest criteria/checklist of score components. It is helpful for students to have an opportunity to review the criteria/outcomes you are looking for in a challenge *before* starting their work.

Some of the best opportunities for challenging students come from mistakes and misconceptions. With a classroom culture in which students feel they can fail without repercussions or can experiment to seek information, you can manifest great gains in understanding. For example, automotive students were tearing apart an engine to confirm why certain parts were worn, only to find their idea was incorrect and that there were different causes. They enjoyed the investigation so much that they asked if they could design an experiment for their peers. Understandably, "getting it right" is important in the world of work and for success on the job, but opportunities to stretch students' thinking and engage their minds are created through "not getting it right," too.

A Roman philosopher, Seneca, asserted, "Difficulties strengthen the mind, as labor does the body." All CTE teachers have opportunities to challenge students through robust, authentic work-related assignments and projects. Assigning challenging work communicates high expectations for your students and acknowledges your belief in their capabilities. Keep in mind that the challenge of an assignment is not just about an unfamiliar task, or a physically demanding task, but also about intellectual demand. Think about which challenges from your field bring a level of complexity: more reasoning, using evidence, involving multistep tasks, and communicating an expectation that students must explain their thinking. These challenges are only part of a wide array of experiences that you can create and get satisfaction from seeing your students learn!

Experiences from the field

Giving effective feedback contributes to student success. It pays to develop different ways to communicate direction and advice that fit your style and work well with your students. Written feedback on assignments, oral feedback while observing students practicing skills, weekly checklists of workplace behaviors you expect in the lab—all of these are helpful to move students forward. Provide personal notes with specific positives and changes for improvement as students enter each day, add comments to their technical journal entries, or have a quick question and answer (Q & A) while in the lab practicing for their credentialing tests.

Keeping students engaged in the classroom may require some different techniques than when they are working in the lab. A quick and nonthreatening way of "taking the temperature" during a theory lesson can include using mini-whiteboards—each student gets a whiteboard and marker to jot down answers to show you. This allows you to see thoughts from every student, not just one or two, when you ask a question of the large group. If budget is a concern, just use blank white paper instead of a whiteboard.

Think about having "mini-conferences" with each of your students on a regular basis. Task each student with organizing what he or she will share  in terms of specific goals, progress, questions, and suggestions on what help is needed. These conferences will give you an opportunity to assess each student and to keep reiterating what it will take to reach targeted goals.

CTE teachers have a wealth of experience on providing feedback and challenging others in the workplace. Your colleagues can be a great resource for techniques and strategies that are working for their students. A business teacher experiments all year with using a blog for students to post entries on project progress and to engage in peer review. She enjoys checking in on the blog and writing her thoughts while reviewing the students' feedback.

Another teacher was having difficulty engaging his students in a challenging project when he presented the activity in a straightforward manner. So instead, he decided to create "an air of urgency" by having a member of his employer advisory committee visit and set forth a challenge to the students. The employer asked students for assistance with a problem that kept occurring at his business. The teacher asked the students to identify what they already knew about the situation/problem and recorded it on a wall. Students were next asked what they wanted to know to help solve the problem, and these questions were posted on the wall. This input (what you know, what you want to know http://teachingstrategies.

pbworks.com/w/page/19940831/KWL%20-%20What%20I%20Know,%20
What%20I%20Want%20to%20Know,%20What%20I%20learned) became part
of their problem-solving wall of ideas and progress. Students then started
researching the questions while identifying more questions and information needed. The business representative visited a week later to learn of
students' progress and provide more information. This authentic problem-solving approach was much more motivating for the students. They
worked as a team and were very excited to present their findings to their
"customer."

KEY POINTS FROM THIS CHAPTER

1. Challenge students through complex, but attainable assignments.
2. Use frequent and specific feedback to support students!
3. Achievable challenges may entail struggles that are important learning experiences.
4. Failures and mistakes are a gold mine of opportunity for learning.
5. Have students uncover mistakes to kick-start motivation.

RELATED CONTENT THAT MAY BE OF INTEREST

Association for Career Technical Education. (2019b). Policy, Advocacy and Research Publications. CTE Publications. Alexandria, VA: Association for Career &Technical Education. Available at https://www. acteonline.org/policy-advocacy-publications/.

MAX Teaching. (2017). Max Teaching Materials: Additional (Free) Resources. Worthington, PA: Max Teaching. Available at http://www. maxteaching.com/teaching-materials.php.

McLeod, S. (2018, May 21). Maslow's hierarchy of needs. Available at www.simplypsychology.org/maslow.html.

PBworks. (2007). KWL - What I Know, What I Want to Know, What I learned. KWL Chart. Available at http://teachingstrategies.pbworks. com/w/page/19940831/KWL%20-%20What%20I%20Know,%20 What%20I%20Want%20to%20Know,%20What%20I%20learned.

Strong, R., Silver, H.F., & Robinson, A. (1995). Strengthening student engagement: What do students want (and what really motivates them)? *Educational Leadership, 53* (1), 8-12. Available at http://www. ascd.org/publications/educational-leadership/sept95/vol53/num01/ Strengthening-Student-Engagement@-What-Do-Students-Want.aspx.

Wees, D. (2012, December 10). 56 Examples of Formative Assessment. Edutopia, George Lucas Educational Foundation. Available at https://www.edutopia.org/groups/assessment/250941.

chapter X
Tracking Student Competence
How Am I Doing?

Tracking competence

Some who are reading this book are reading it from cover to cover. Some are picking out chapters based on their interest in the titles. Still others are highlighting and writing margin notes of discussion items for the next pre-service professional development day.

When you have been involved in education as long as the authors of this book, you see a number of trends gain and lose popularity. These trends are similar to waves on an ocean. They come in strong and then they fade away; some stay longer than others, but all have an impact which remains some part of the education landscape. Altogether, there have been a lot of waves.

One of those waves concerns the use of grading in education. Is grading positive or negative; something that assists student learning; a distractor; something that improves a student's self-esteem; or something that tears it down? Those issues will not be tackled here, but it is an important opportunity to highlight something that is usually a distinction between CTE teachers and regular education teachers. That distinction is the separation between grades (as referred to by most of the education community) and competency tracking.

Though CTE teachers work in different institutions that have different policies, the reality is that most will have to determine an overall evaluation for students' learning, almost always in the form of a letter grade. Competency tracking is something different. As you know from your experiences in the workplace, competence is generally based on one's knowledge and skills, and on the ability to apply these in a variety of different settings. People advance in a technical field based on their knowledge and skills. The same is true in CTE, except that for students, it is at a much more basic level.

Your students will need the basic knowledge and skills required to be competent in their profession, but they also need the skill set to help them advance. How do we know if they have the ability to do that? A teacher must verify it piece by piece, as a student develops each skill. Generally, technical skills build on one another; one skill is a building block toward another. Often you can't complete step three without successful completion of steps two and one.

Unlike grading, often viewed as on a continuum, tracking competencies is more of a black and white issue based on a task analysis. Can your student successfully perform a mitered corner on every attempt? By the way, a mitered corner is a term used in a variety of occupations; it involves beveling two pieces of material to form a corner around something else. In carpentry it could be around a window or a door; in commercial art it may be a frame around a picture; or in plumbing it may be the angle at which you cut plastic piping to avoid the piping getting in the way of something else. All those examples assume that making a mitered angle requires other skill sets, such as proper measurement, cutting-tool choice, cutting- tool use, an ability to adjust the angle, an understanding of the material, and so forth. Many of those skills should be tracked along the way.

In most cases, this tracking moves from simple to complex and usually involves clusters of tasks determined by analyzing the occupation. As an example, one cluster might involve the use of hand-operated tools, and the subtasks may include measuring, cutting, shaping, and drilling. Each task will involve meeting some goal or rubric that is used for some form of evaluation on the CTE teacher's part; the evaluation may or may not require a grade.

In the earlier days of CTE, this competency tracking often took the form of a competency chart, and in some cases the charts were public. In other words, the charts were hung on a bulletin board so that members of the class could see how they were progressing. Some would argue that using a public chart creates an unhealthy competition among class members. That is a determination you will have to make for yourself. In addition to the decision on public versus private, you will also need to make some determination on format, media, grade versus checkmark, and a few other things you can talk to your mentors and supervisors about. Whether or not to track competencies is not a decision for a CTE teacher; however, the teacher may have some input as to the process and format.

One last comment related to competency data and student success should be mentioned. At this writing almost all schools delivering CTE are transitioning from funding through the federal Perkins IV legislation, noted earlier, to funding through the recently enacted Perkins V (Strengthening Career and Technical Education for the 21st Century Act). Under the new legislation, all state and local CTE programs are required to participate in a needs assessment every two years. The data acquired from the needs assessment will be used to drive program expenditures for secondary, postsecondary, and adult students who participate in CTE courses.

Current student competency level data can provide valuable insight as to the ongoing success of the CTE programs being offered. A student's eventual success in his or her chosen field will reflect on the comprehensiveness and the quality of the training that the student received. You'll want to know that your students received the best education you can provide; you'll want to be able to track that progress; and you'll want to use student competency data to help drive ongoing program improvement!

An easy way for new CTE teachers to begin to track an individual student's skills is to find the listing of standards that his or her program is required to complete. These competencies could come from a variety of sources including a state's department of CTE, which may have a mandatory listing of competencies for a variety of occupations, or they could be standards developed by the local school district and aligned to state curriculum frameworks. A state's department of licensure may list requirements to achieve a credential (e.g., nurse aide), or you may be using an industry standard (e.g., Manufacturing Skill Standards Council, [MSSC]), the O*NET standards, or a national credential provider's blueprint (e.g., NOCTI). Assuming the list is not proprietary, you may be able to simply copy the selected standards for each student, or you may have to break the standards down into the granular steps needed to obtain them, as discussed above. You can make these documents part of your grade book (either physical or electronic), or you could keep them on a clipboard as you monitor and evaluate your students.

Experiences from the field

A teacher might use competency checklists and list all students in columns on one sheet. In this case, after a particular student completes a skill, the teacher gains a comparative view of how the entire class is progressing.

As mentioned earlier, another option would be to utilize a classroom display of the competencies to be achieved. Though this does have some connotations of competitiveness, it also may have some benefits. It enables students to see the totality of what they need to be competent and how they are progressing toward it. Students are also able to see which classmates they can talk to for help, because the chart will show which students have competency in an area of concern. If you choose the option of a public display, think also about ways you can use it to build additional skills. If you are a drafting, commercial art, or information technology teacher, designing the chart could become a small project. If there are no state or school policies regarding competency tracking, try to talk to a mentor teacher or supervisor about this topic.

With a national emphasis on implementing POS, defined earlier as a coordinated, non-duplicative sequence of technical and academic courses that aligns secondary and postsecondary education and features in both Perkins IV and Perkins V legislation, a number of states have standardized their POS statewide. We know a veteran CTE teacher from one of these states who has incorporated the state-required competencies into his program and monitors his students' progress through those required competencies. These competencies also align with the national industry credential as well as the state-required end-of-program assessment. This represents an ideally aligned system that can benefit both the student and the CTE teacher.

This teacher has researched classroom management systems and spoken to peers regarding competency tracking. He tried to gather as many good examples as possible and used this as his starting point. This savvy CTE teacher, who happens to be involved in the culinary industry, was able to form an assessment style and tracking system that works with state POS requirements and industry standards, and gives his students the best feedback to achieve success. He uses rubrics to build students' skills from simple to complex, which simultaneously builds the students' confidence and pride in workmanship. Evaluation against these rubrics is entered into the school's computer system. In addition, pictures of student projects are also entered and stored with information about student competency progress. Once a student has achieved competency, the achievement is documented, added to the "master" competency task list, and is placed into the student's portfolio.

This process of rubrics, competency sign-offs, and portfolios all culminates in a series of final end-of-the-year projects. This final assessment includes: NOCTI written and practical exams, a group catering event, and a formal presentation of students' restaurant/pastry project, all of which are on display and open to the public for viewing. By building skills/competencies into a portfolio, the students have an excellent tool to showcase their work to future college admission representatives and at job interviews.

Another example comes to us from the state of Virginia. The Virginia Department of Education has required tracking and maintenance of student competency records for many years. The Commonwealth offered templates and spreadsheets through its state CTE Resource Center. In the 2012-13 school year, the Commonwealth of Virginia began voluntary implementation of CanDo, an online competency tracking system developed for teachers through a collaboration of partners within the state. Taking advantage of Virginia's state-approved task/competency lists, CanDo allows educators to track students' progress electronically.

The system is built on open-source software and can be set up and implemented in any school division, regardless of size. The CTE Resource Center provides technical support and training for implementing the system. Though the system is based on one state's set of standards, anyone can view its operation by going to http://cando.cteresource.org/teacher_resources/Project.mp4. For the 2018-19 school year. As of 2013, approximately are utilizing the program across their CTE programs. The system has the ability to show a variety of views, such as percentages of completion within a cluster of skills, and project completion.

KEY POINTS FROM THIS CHAPTER

1. Competency verification and grading are not the same.
2. Evaluate student competence.
3. Competencies are like building blocks.
4. Know your program's standards.
5. Consider the format, media, and privacy of your system carefully.

RELATED CONTENT THAT MAY BE OF INTEREST

CareerOneStop. (2019b). *Competency Model Clearinghouse*. Washington, DC: US Department of Labor, Employment and Training Administration. Available at https://www.careeronestop.org/CompetencyModel/.

Carl D. Perkins Career and Technical Education Act Of 2006, Public Law 88—210; December 18, 1963. As Amended Through P.L. 116—6, and enacted February 15, 2019, is known as The Strengthening Career and Technical Education for the 21st Century Act or Perkins V. available at https://legcounsel.house.gov/Comps/Carl%20D.%20Perkins%20Career%20And%20Technical%20Education%20Act%20Of%202006(not-in-effect).pdf.

Carl D. Perkins Career and Technical Education Improvement Act of 2006, Public Law 109-270, section 113:2:A:v.

Hodes, C.L., Foster, J., & Pritz, S.G. (2019). *Putting your data to work, 3rd ed*. Alexandria VA: ACTE. Available at www.acteonline.org.

James-Ward, C., Fisher, D. Frey, N., & Lapp, D. (2013). *Using data to focus instructional improvement*. Alexandria, VA: ASCD. Available at http://www.ascd.org/Publications/Books/Overview/Using-Data-to-Focus-Instructional-Improvement.aspx.

Virginia Department of Education. Career Clusters: Virginia's Educational Resource System Online (VERSO). Available at http://cteresource.org/verso/categories/across-the-board.

Conclusion

We know that CTE teachers are a special breed; we've said it in this book many times, and in other books and articles we've published. There are numerous differences between these educators and other traditionally prepared educators—differences in prior work experience, work environments, and operating a safe environment for students to learn. Although there are many books on teaching strategies, with quite a few focused on tips for new teachers, we are aware of none focused on new CTE teachers who have come primarily from alternative certification programs. We hope this book begins to address a CTE community need for a short and simple, focused but lighthearted resource that focuses on helping the new CTE teacher. We hope you find the chapter titles intriguing and humorous, but more than that we hope you find them useful. As we have done with previous chapters, we wanted to also provide you with a list of key points for the overall book, so in no particular order, here we go!

- Get to know your students, because that knowledge directly impacts a student's ability to succeed.
- Learn how to stay current as an educator.
- Knowing that you care about a student's career success is a huge student motivator.
- A CTE teacher is part career coach, part teacher, and part mentor.
- Safety is critical in any lab environment, especially one that includes 20 novices who believe they can't be hurt.
- Find ways of establishing student buy-in; help students direct as much of their own learning as possible.
- Be a role model for your students through your actions, behaviors, and choices.
- Dynamic lesson planning is key to success.
- Develop a support system; include colleagues, administrators, counselors, experienced teachers, and your occupational advisory committee members.
- Become part of the larger professional community; join ACTE.
- Students appreciate knowing your expectations and it helps them to succeed.
- Develop your own way to challenge students in the classroom and in the lab/shop/clinic.
- Establish a system that tracks student competence and keep it up to date.

The authors and the contributing authors really hope you find this book useful and that you will consider reviewing the new CTE Teacher courses available at www.ctelearn.org.

Contributing Authors

The authors would like to both recognize and thank the following individuals for their contributions to this book. These individuals provided content for "Experiences from the field" along with a variety of expertise regarding many topics throughout this book. These individuals are not only experts, but they are also dedicated to CTE and its continuous improvement. We are proud to call them both colleagues and friends.

Bryan D. Albrecht, Ed. D.
Gateway Technical College, Wisconsin

Gregory G. Belcher, Ph.D.
Pittsburg State University, Technical Teacher Education, Kansas

Alisha Hyslop, Ph.D.
Association for Career and Technical Education, Virginia

Lynda Jackson
Mason County Area Technology Center, Kentucky

Joanna Kister, Ph.D.
Education and Workforce Development, Kister Consulting Services, Florida

Michelle R. Oliveira, M.Ed.
Career Technical Education Leadership and Instructional Support Office, California

Brian D. Peffley, CEPC, CCE, AAC
Lebanon County Career and Technology Center, Pennsylvania

Marie P. Perotti, B.S.
Colton Redlands Yucaipa Regional Occupational Program,
CTE TEACH, Program Manager, California

Cathy B. Sroka, M. Ed.
Educational Administration Consultant, Pennsylvania

Contributing Organizations

The authors would like to both recognize and thank ACTE and NOCTI for their contributions and assistance with this book. Unlike the individuals recognized in the previous section, these entities provided the authors with the opportunity to expand their individual knowledge and skills and have indirectly influenced much of the content of this book through conversations and interviews with their members and clients. In addition, these organizations have contributed resources, both human and financial, to make this book a reality.

ACTE (The Association for Career and Technical Education)
The Association for Career and Technical Education is the largest national education association in the United States and is dedicated to the advancement of education that prepares youth and adults for careers. ACTE was founded in 1926, and it remains committed to enhancing the job performance and satisfaction of its members; to increasing public awareness and appreciation for career and technical education (CTE); and to assuring growth in local, state, and federal funding for these programs by communicating and working with legislators and government leaders.

NOCTI (formerly the National Occupational Competency Testing Institute)
NOCTI is an assessment organization that was founded in the mid-sixties as a not-for-profit entity serving the CTE field through a consortium made up of career technical education directors (or their designees) from each state and U.S. territory. NOCTI shares the objective of other CTE associations, including Advance CTE, who elect the NOCTI board of directors, and the Association for Career and Technical Educators (ACTE), whose membership this book is targeted to assist. All three organizations have expertise in, and a strong commitment to, improving America's workforce.

Special Thanks

Amie L. Bloomfield, B.S., NOCTI, Executive Vice President
for additional editing and creative thought process

Carol L. Hodes, Ph.D., NOCTI, Senior Consultant
for searching the literature for resources that are useful to CTE teachers

Jaclyn D. Lenger, NOCTI, Graphic Designer
for her creative illustrations and suggestions

Sandra G. Pritz, Ph.D., NOCTI Senior Consultant
for many hours spent checking consistency, tone, style, and grammar.

Complete Resource List

Association for Career Technical Education. (2019a). *Career and technical student organizations*. Alexandria, VA: ACTE. Available at https://www.acteonline.org/professional-development/high-quality-cte-tools/career-and-technical-student-organizations/.

Association for Career Technical Education. (2019b). Policy, Advocacy and Research Publications. CTE Publications. Alexandria, VA: Association for Career &Technical Education. Available at https://www.acteonline.org/policy-advocacy-publications/.

Beall, G. (2017, November 6). Eight Key differences between Gen Z and Millennials. Verizon Media, Huffpost. Available at https://www.huffpost.com/entry/8-key-differences-between_b_12814200.

Bottoms, G. & Phillips, I. (2010). *Skills for a lifetime: Teaching students the habits of success.* Atlanta, GA: Southern Regional Education Board. Available at https://www.sreb.org/sites/main/files/file-attachments/10v25_skills_for_a_lifetime_intro.pdf.

Bybee, R.W., Buchwald, C. E., Crissman, S., Heil, D. R., Kuerbis, P. J., Matsumoto, C., & McInerney, J. D. (1989). *Science and technology education for the elementary years: Frameworks for curriculum and instruction.* Washington, D.C.: Office of Educational Research and Improvement (ED). Available at https://eric.ed.gov/?id=ED314237.

CareerOneStop. (2019a). *Generic Building Blocks Competency Model.* Washington, DC: US Department of Labor, Employment and Training Administration. Available at https://www.careeronestop.org/CompetencyModel/competency-models/building-blocks-model.aspx.

CareerOneStop. (2019b). *Competency Model Clearinghouse.* Washington, DC: US Department of Labor, Employment and Training Administration. Available at https://www.careeronestop.org/CompetencyModel/.

Carl D. Perkins Career and Technical Education Act Of 2006, Public Law 88–210; December 18, 1963. As Amended Through P.L. 116–6, and enacted February 15, 2019, is known as The Strengthening Career and Technical Education for the 21st Century Act or Perkins V. available at https://legcounsel.house.gov/Comps/Carl%20D.%20Perkins%20Career%20And%20Technical%20Education%20Act%20Of%202006(not-in-effect).pdf.

Carl D. Perkins Career and Technical Education Improvement Act of 2006, Public Law 109-270, section 113:2:A:v.

Carney, P., Crilley, E., Fala, J.T., Strouse, K., Tully, C., & Viviano, T. (2013). In-classroom coach: An addition to mentor teachers. *Techniques, (88)* 7, 50-55. Available at http://www.nxtbook.com/ygsreprints/ACTE/g36681_acte_techniques_oct2013/#/50.

Carr, J. & Bertrando, S. (2012). Top 10 instructional strategies for struggling students. *Leadership, 42* (1), 24-26, 38. Available at http://eric.ed.gov/?id=EJ983557.

Chen, D. & McGeehan, P. (2012, May 1). Social media rules limit student-teacher contact. *The New York Times,* p.20. Available at https://www.nytimes.com/2012/05/02/nyregion/social-media-rules-for-nyc-school-staff-limits-contact-with-students.html.

Danielson, C. (2008). *The handbook for enhancing professional practice.* Alexandria, VA: ASCD.

Department of Career and Technical Education. (2019, March 6). *Program advisory committee guide.* Bismarck, ND: North Dakota Department of Education. Available at https://www.cte.nd.gov/sites/www/files/documents/Budget%20%26%20Finance/State-Carl%20Perkins/AdvisoryCommitteeGuide.pdf.

Education Writers Association & William and Flora Hewlett Foundation. (2017). *Decoding Deeper Learning in the Classroom.* Washington, DC: Education Writers Association. Available at https://files.eric.ed.gov/fulltext/ED581546.pdf.

Faculty Development and Instructional Design Center. (2015). A Tutorial on Faculty Student Relationships: Balancing Roles and Maintaining Boundaries. DeKalb, Il: Northern Illinois University College of Education. Available at https://www.niu.edu/facdev/resources/relationships/presentation.html.

Fink, J. L. W. (2014). No-sweat lesson prep. *Instructor, 123(5),* 45-47. Available at http:// https://www.scholastic.com/teachers/articles/teaching-content/no-sweat-lesson-prep/.

Fiscus, L. (ed) & Hyslop, A. (2008). Career and technical student organizations reference guide. Leesburg, VA: SkillsUSA. Available at https://www.skillsusa.org/wp-content/uploads/2014/12/CTSOs-a-Reference-Guide.pdf.

Fritsch, J. M. (2014). Beyond the workshop. *Techniques, (89)5,* 16-19. Available at https://www.acteonline.org/publications/techniques/techniques-archives/.

Guido, M. (2017, March 2). The Guide to Cooperative Learning: Principles and Strategies for Each Type. Teaching Strategies Blog. Available at https://www.prodigygame.com/blog/cooperative-learning-principles-st.

Hake, K. (2009). Career Activities and Vocational Lesson Plans. Vocational Information Center. Available at http://www.khake.com/page94.html.

Harbin, B. & Bottoms, G. (2008). *Planning for improved student achievement.* Atlanta, GA: Southern Regional Education Board. Available at https://www.sreb.org/sites/main/files/file-attachments/08v05_sbu_intro.pdf.

Hodes, C.L., Foster, J., & Pritz, S.G. (2019). *Putting your data to work, 3rd ed.* Alexandria VA: ACTE. Available at www.acteonline.org.

James-Ward, C., Fisher, D. Frey, N., & Lapp, D. (2013). *Using data to focus instructional improvement.* Alexandria, VA: ASCD. Available at http://www.ascd.org/Publications/Books/Overview/Using-Data-to-Focus-Instructional-Improvement.aspx.

Kosloski, M. (2014, February). Making CTE work through CTSOs. *Techniques, 89*(2), 34-37. Available at http://www.nxtbook.com/ygsreprints/ACTE/g39344_acte_feb2014/index. php?startid=34.

Lieber, C. M. (2009). *Getting classroom management right: Guided discipline and personalized support in secondary schools.* Cambridge, MA: Educators for Social Responsibility. Accessed September 9, 2019 at https://positiveclassroomrelationships.weebly.com/worksheets.html.

Massachusetts Department of Education. (2008). *A toolkit for new teachers.* Lexington, MA: Minuteman Regional Vocational Technical School District. Available at http://www.tantasqua.org/superintendent/teachingandlearning/docs/helpfullinks/ NewTeacherToolkit2008.pdf.

MAX Teaching. (2017). Max Teaching Materials: Additional (Free) Resources. Worthington, PA: Max Teaching. Available at http://www.maxteaching.com/teaching-materials.php.

McLeod, S. (2018, May 21). Maslow's hierarchy of needs. Available at www.simplypsychology.org/maslow.html.

Mentor Michigan. (n.d.). *Michigan State Government mentoring guidelines.* Available at http://www.michigan.gov/documents/Mentor_Guidelines_101422_7.pdf.

Michigan Department of Education. (2019, August). *Program advisory committee tool kit.* Lansing, MI: Office of Career and Technical Education. Available at https://www. michigan.gov/documents/mde/Program_Advisory_Tool_Kit_2017_597534_7.pdf.

National Academy of Sciences, National Academy of Engineering and Institute of Medicine. (1997). *Adviser, teacher, role model, friend: On being a mentor to students in science and engineering.* Washington, DC: The National Academies Press. Available at https://www.nap. edu/read/5789/chapter/1.

National Association of State Directors of Teacher Education and Certification. (2015). Model Code of Ethics for Educators (MCEE). Washington, DC: NASDTEC. Available at https://www.nasdtec.net/page/MCEE_Doc.

National Center for O*NET Development. (2019). O*NET Career Exploration Tools. Washington, DC: US Department of Labor. Available at https://www.onetcenter.org/tools. html O*Net Interest Profiler.

NASA. (n.d.). The 5E instructional model. *NASA eClips.* Available at https://nasaeclips.arc. nasa.gov/teachertoolbox/the5e#collapseOne.

NIOSH. (2003). Safety checklist program for schools. DHHS (NIOSH) Publication Number 2004-101. Washington, DC: Author. Available at http://www.cdc.gov/niosh/ docs/2004-101/resources.html.

OSHA. (2011). Laboratory Safety Electrical Hazards. OSHA Quick Facts. Washington, DC: Occupational Safety and Health Administration. Available at https://www.osha.gov/ Publications/laboratory/OSHAquickfacts-lab-safety-electrical-hazards.pdf.

OSHA newsletter subscription: Available at https://www.osha.gov/as/opa/quicktakes/ qtpostcard.html.

Pace University (2014, August). *Wood & Finishing Shop Safety Plan.* NY, NY: PACE University Environmental Health and Safety. Available at https://www.pace.edu/sites/default/files/files/wood-finishing-shop-safety-plan.pdf.

Partnership for 21st Century Learning. (2019). *Framework for 21st Century Learning.* Columbus, OH: Battelle for Kids. Available at http://static.battelleforkids.org/documents/p21/P21_Framework_Brief.pdf.

Pawlowski, B. (2014). Backyard advocacy—How local business partners can help. *Techniques, (89)3, 34-37.*

Payne, R. (2008). Nine powerful practices. *Educational Leadership, 65*(7), 48-52. Available at http://www.ascd.org/publications/educational-leadership/apr08/vol65/num07/Nine-Powerful-Practices.aspx.

PBworks. (2007). KWL - What I Know, What I Want to Know, What I learned. KWL Chart. Available at http://teachingstrategies.pbworks.com/w/page/19940831/KWL%20-%20 What%20I%20Know,%20What%20I%20Want%20to%20Know,%20What%20I%20learned

Perna, M. (2006). Making the connection. *Techniques, (81)8,* 42-43. Available at https://eric.ed.gov/?q=Perna&ff1=dtySince_2000&ff2=autPerna%2c+Mark+C.&id= EJ751462.

Reading Quest. (2018). A to Z List of Strategies. Available at http://www.readingquest. org/a-z-strategies.html.

Rhodes, J. (2011). Research corner: Ethical principles for youth mentoring relationships. *MENTOR.* National Mentoring Partnership: Alexandria, VA. Available at http://files.eric.ed.gov/fulltext/ED522075.pdf.

Rice, C. (2012). *Creative strategies for CTE teachers* (NC CTE Comprehensive Support Model). Available at http://scotlandcte.files.wordpress.com/2012/08/creative-strategies-handbook.pdf.

Safety Culture. (2019). Safety Culture: 5S Plus Safety. St Louis MO: Safety Culture. Available at https://safetyculture.com/topics/6s-lean/.

Saavedra, A.R. & Opfer, D. V. (2012, October 24). Nine lessons on how to teach 21st century skills. *Education Week, (32)* 9. Available at http://www.rand.org/blog/2012/10/nine-lessons-on-how-to-teach-21st-century-skills-and.html.

Schroer, W.J. (n.d.). Generations X, Y, Z and the others. *The Social Librarian.* http://www.socialmarketing.org/newsletter/features/generation3.htm.

Schroer, D. (2014). Top five local advocacy tips for success. *Techniques, (89)*3, 38-41.

SREB. (2013, May). *Counseling for careers can connect students to a goal beyond high school graduation.* Newsletter of Best Practices from the 26th annual High Schools That Work Staff Development Conference, New Orleans, LA. Atlanta, GA: SREB. Available at https://www.sreb.org/sites/main/files/file-attachments/13v08w_bestpractices_counseling.pdf.

SREB. (2016, July 28). *Guidance and Strategies Needed to Jump-Start College and Careers.* Newsletter of Best Practices from the 29th annual High Schools That Work Staff Development Conference, Atlanta, GA. Atlanta, GA: SREB. Available at https://www.sreb.org/post/best-practices-2015-hstw-staff-development-conference.

Strong, R., Silver, H.F., & Robinson, A. (1995). Strengthening student engagement: What do students want (and what really motivates them)? *Educational Leadership, 53* (1), 8-12. Available at http://www.ascd.org/publications/educational-leadership/sept95/vol53/num01/Strengthening-Student-Engagement@-What-Do-Students-Want.aspx.

Terada, Y. (2019, August 7). 8 Proactive Classroom Management Tips. Lucas Education Research. Available at https://www.edutopia.org/article/8-proactive-classroom-management-tips.

The Learning System. (2013, Summer). Creating Norms. Oxford, OH: Learning Forward. Available at https://learningforward.org/docs/default-source/learning-system/ls-sum13-creating-norms-tool.pdf.

The National Coordinating Council for Career and Technical Student Organizations (NCC-CTSO). (2019). *Career Technical Student Organizations.* Available at http://www.ctsos.org/.

US Consumer Safety Product Commission. (2006). *School Chemistry Laboratory Safety Guide.* Washington, DC: Department of Health and Human Services. Available at www.cdc.gov/niosh/docs/2007-107/pdfs/2007-107.pdf.

Virginia Department of Education. (n.d.). Career Clusters: Virginia's Educational Resource System Online (VERSO). Available at http://cteresource.org/verso/categories/across-the-board.

Virginia's CTE Resource Center. (n.d.). Virginia's Educational Resource System Online: Course Task/Competency Lists and Other Resources. Henrico, VA: Virginia Department of Education. Available at http://www.cteresource.org/verso/.

Wees, D. (2012, December 10). 56 Examples of Formative Assessment. Edutopia, George Lucas Educational Foundation. Available at https://www.edutopia.org/groups/assessment/250941.

Westerberg, T. (2013, September 17). *Instructional leadership: Walking the talk.* InService Blog. Alexandria, VA: ASCD Available at http://inservice.ascd.org/books/instructional-leadership-walking-the-talk/.

West Virginia Department of Education. (n.d.). Simulated Workplace. Available at http://wvde.state.wv.us/simulated-workplace/.

Wood, C., Porter, D., Brady, K. & Forton, M. (2003). Everyday rules that really work! *Scholastic Teacher Magazine, 113*(1), 25. Available at http://www.scholastic.com/teachers/article/everyday-rules-really-work.

Zirkle, C. (2013). Don't let legal issues put you in hot water! A safety and liability primer. *Tech Directions, 72*(6) 17-23. Available at http://www.omagdigital.com/publication/?i=139140